What *is* a Googly?

Robert Eastaway went to school in Chester and graduated in engineering at Christ's College, Cambridge. In 1986 he co-invented the Deloittes computer world ratings for cricket, which are now called the Coopers & Lybrand Ratings. He is a consultant and lecturer on creative thinking, and spends his weekends playing cricket – he is one of those bowlers who rub the ball on their trousers.

Mark Stevens was educated at Harrow. (The local comprehensive and sixth form college, not the other one.) He is a graphic artist and illustrator in London. Although he is an avid cricket spectator, he rarely plays. He can't bowl googlies – but his dad can.

What *is* a Googly?

The Mysteries of Cricket Explained

Robert Eastaway

Illustrations by Mark Stevens

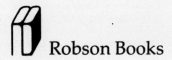 Robson Books

This book is dedicated to the tea-makers, without whom the Mandarins Cricket Club could not survive.

First published in Great Britain in 1992 by Robson Books Ltd, Bolsover House, 5-6 Clipstne Street, London W1P 7EB

Copyright © 1992 Robert Eastaway
The right of Robert Eastaway to be identified as author of this work has been asserted by him in accordance with the Copyright, Designs and Patents Act 1988

British Library Cataloguing-in-Publication Data
A catalogue record for this book is available from the British Library

ISBN 0 86051 800 0

Typeset by Spectrum Typesetting Ltd., London.
Printed by Butler & Tanner Ltd., London and Frome

Contents

Acknowledgements

I am most grateful to the many people – including my dental hygienist and my plumber – who confessed to me the questions that they had always wanted to ask about cricket.

Thanks to Linda O'Shea, and to fellow Mandarins Mike O'Shea, Mike Richardson and Paul McIntyre; also to Chris Roles, Neil Gregory, Fedelma Morris, David Flavell, Lesley Stevenson, Roger Maile, Jane Rodger and Joanna Griffiths for taking the time to review and comment in detail on the many early drafts of this book.

In the closing stages, Derek Lodge's cricket knowledge and library were invaluable, and John Holmstrom, Leo McKinstry, James Perry, Stephen Green and Ron Quibell also generously helped me out at short notice.

Finally, I am indebted to Cheryl the Cheerleader (for coming with me to Lord's on a freezing day); and most of all to Rachael Heyhoe Flint, Matthew Engel, Charlotte Howard, Mrs McLean and Sarah Woodgate-Jones who provided the moral support when it was needed most.

Foreword by
Ted Dexter

A great many cricket books are published every year for those who know and love the game. This book is quite different: it is designed primarily for those who have no knowledge or understanding of cricket. So when Robert first told me that I was the ideal person to write the Foreword to such a book, I had to wonder whether this could have been better phrased ...

There are people, of course, who are quite certain that the men who select the England cricket team (myself included) know nothing about the game. On that logic, this would be an ideal volume for a Selector. I suspect however that in reality its appeal will go rather wider. This is not to say that cricket's administrators have nothing to learn. Few who know anything about cricket would claim to know everything about it; that is part of cricket's eternal appeal.

Cricket attracts a huge following. In this country and abroad, many thousands derive immense enjoyment from all the different aspects of the game – playing it, watching it, listening to it on radio, and reading and talking about it. I include myself in all these categories, although my own playing days – short of some extraordinary aberration on the part of the Selectors – are now well and truly over.

The essential point here of course is that you do not need to be fortunate enough to play at the highest level to realize how infinitely rich cricket's appeal is. The pleasure that individuals derive from cricket – or indeed the seriousness with which they view the game – has no correlation with their own playing standards. That is another aspect of the game's attraction.

For this is not a book simply about first class or Test cricket; it is about cricket the game, which means cricket at all levels. Lord's cricket ground has its unique qualities, as does the village green. Both have their role in the game. But it is not necessary to go to Lord's – still less to play there – in order to begin to appreciate something of cricket's richness and variety, its physical and mental challenges, its triumphs and disasters, its comedy and ironies…

My good wishes go to all those who, like me, believe they might still have something to learn about our national game – but especially to those who think they have everything to learn about our national game. And to the latter I should add a word of warning: this book might be the start of a life-long addiction.

Ted Dexter.

The Team

1

Why This Book?

Some time ago I was having a drink with an American friend. He had spent the afternoon half-watching a game of cricket on Kew Green and I asked him what he'd made of it. He said that there were a lot of things that he didn't understand (which turned out to be an understatement), but in particular he couldn't grasp two things: why were all the players wearing white (didn't they all have terrible laundry bills each week)?; and why were they all prepared to stand around for so long without doing anything?

My American friend is not alone in being rather baffled by cricket. In fact the majority of people that I have talked with since have – with a little coaxing – confessed to having 'one or two' questions about cricket that they have always been too embarrassed to ask. Highly popular on the list were: 'What exactly *is* a silly mid off?' and 'What *is* a googly?' And it seems that half the United Kingdom is anxious to know the answer to: 'Why *do* they rub the ball on their trousers?'

Those large numbers who play cricket every weekend, however, seem to take it for granted that their families, friends and work colleagues will somehow 'understand' its importance. 'I'm sorry, darling, but you'll have to entertain the Browns on your own this weekend because I'm playing cricket.' 'Sorry, Bill, I can't make the merger talks on Wednesday, we're playing against the Old Woodleighans.'

Of course, those who are not addicted to cricket don't necessarily understand this obsession, partly because nobody has tried to explain the game. Nobody, that is, except the inventor of that tea-towel which can be found in many of the kitchens of Great Britain, and which pretends to explain cricket to Americans.

Has it ever occurred to cricketers that the only reason most of their wives come along to the game is that it is marginally preferable to be able to see your other half at 100 yards than not to see him at all? And that the remote, glazed look that comes over them when the cricketer is explaining his catch at silly mid off is not one of admiration but of incomprehension (and boredom)?

Well, this book is an attempt to uncover the freemasonry of cricket so that those who want to can get a better understanding of what it is that so obsesses the millions of cricket lovers all over the world. I have tried to explain *why* it is that people get so passionate about cricket. Perhaps it will take more than a book to convince a newcomer to the game. But I hope at least that it will sow a seed which, after further study and not a little patience, could just convert one or two people.

The chapters are all based on the questions that I have been asked most often – by Spanish, Irish, American and Scottish folk as well as by the English. The book is designed to be read straight through, but you can dip in to it to answer particular questions. The first time that I have used a bit of cricket jargon, I have underlined it – and of course, if you are ever confused by a word, you can always look it up in the glossary.

The glossary may seem a bit long, but I thought it was better to include too much than to have too little, because cricket abounds with technical terms. What is particularly confusing is that there is often more than one term to describe something in cricket – and often you will hear a commentator using all of them in one sentence. For example, those three sticks behind the batsman are called either the stumps or the wicket.

Just to confuse matters even further, there are also some words that mean more than one thing: the wicket is not only those three sticks, but also the dismissal of a batsman (as in 'I took his wicket') and the strip of short-cut grass in the middle of the field (which is also called the pitch). So, it is possible for you to be playing on an uneven 'wicket' (pitch) which means that the ball keeps low and hits your 'wicket' (stumps) thus resulting in the loss of another 'wicket' (man out) for your team. Like any terminology which is new to you, you will probably find all this baffling at first. You might also find it amusing or just plain ridiculous. But you will get used to it remarkably quickly. Remember, cricket is a richly funny game, and its language is part of the great joke.

Cricket is dominated by members of the male sex. At least eighty per cent of spectators, ninety-nine per cent of players, and 100 per cent of the members in the Lord's pavilion are men. I use that as my tame justification for referring to 'he' in the book when 'she' might also apply. I have made no attempt to use terms like 'batswoman' or even 'batsperson', not least because women tend to call themselves batsmen anyway. I hope that, if I need to be, I am forgiven.

Finally, if at any time you find yourself asking the question 'Yes, but *why* do they do that?', remember that cricket and logic don't always go hand in hand: cricketers talk about fair play, but as you will see, in many cases cricket can be as cruel and unfair as it is possible to be.

Cricket is a beautiful and fascinating game. All I have to do now is prove it.

2

Where Did Cricket Come From?

Before we get on to the subject of what cricket is, it's probably worth your while knowing a bit about where it came from, because commentators and others do refer an awful lot to cricket in the 'old days'. Where exactly cricket came from is one of its great mysteries. Perhaps it was first played in a wind-swept field by a couple of bored English shepherds in the fourteenth century. One of the shepherds held a crook, the other a stone. The stone was hurled, and the first shepherd, standing in front of a

wicket gate, 'crooked it'. Well, it's one of the many theories anyway.

Whatever happened, by the eighteenth century 'cricket' was being played all over the countryside, and had even been adopted as a pastime for the gentry, who found it to be an excellent excuse for gambling. And so you had the rich people with the money to gamble, and some rough-necks who were quite happy to be the subject of gambling if it meant that they could earn a few quid. The upper classes and the lower classes suddenly found that they could be happily playing sport on the same field – quite something in such a class-ridden country. Lordly amateurs and more mercenary professionals, the 'gentlemen' and the 'players', were to set the tone of cricket for centuries to come.

Where do Lord's and the MCC come in?

In 1787 a snooty cricketing bunch known as the White Conduit Club decided that they would prefer to play cricket on a private ground near to the fashionable West End of London, rather than the public field they used in Islington. The man who bought the land in Marylebone which suited their purposes was an entrepreneur called Thomas Lord. The club became Marylebone Cricket Club (MCC), they played at Mr Lord's ground and, Bob's-your-uncle, the cricket establishment was born.

It is pure coincidence that many of the first people to play at Lord's really *were* lords. What it meant was that they were important (and arrogant) enough to decide that their version of cricket was the official version, and they wrote the Laws down in 1788. Amazingly, the Laws have hardly changed to this day, although the style of play and some of the words used certainly have.

When did cricket become 'modern'?

In Thomas Lord's time, the bowler threw the ball underarm. But because so much of cricket was about gambling, certain players liked to cheat. First, in 1807, a man from Sussex tried hurling the ball with his arm horizontal; then later certain fellows were to be found bowling with their arm above the shoulder. Such incidents nearly led to riots: cricket was taken just as seriously then as it is now. Eventually the whiskered gentry at the MCC were forced to change the Laws to allow overarm bowling (but it had to be with

17

a straight arm), and underarm bowling quickly died out. In fact, as recently as 1981 a professional bowler did bowl underarm to good effect: Australian Trevor Chappell rolled the last ball of the match along the ground to prevent New Zealand from winning. But although this was strictly legal, it was deemed to be contrary to the spirit of the game and created such an international scandal that these days the only place you are likely to see underarm bowling is on the beach.

In cricket's early days, the players tended to wear breeches or stockings made of <u>flannel</u> (and often white), which were fashionable at the time. By the mid-1800s fashions had changed, and cricketers were wearing white cotton trousers and shirts. In most modern forms of cricket, this white-trouser tradition has stuck, and they are still called flannels.

In 1866, an eighteen-year-old called W G Grace scored 224 runs for All-England against Surrey. He became a cricketing sensation, and arguably the most famous man in Victorian England. Suddenly thousands of people flocked to watch cricket, as long as W G was playing. Thanks to the railways, Grace and his fellow cricketing stars could play all over the country. Cricket has attracted big crowds ever since (although they aren't as big now as they used to be, perhaps because it costs a bit more than a shilling to get in these days).

---

5 OTHER ACTIVITIES ON LORD'S CRICKET GROUND

● 1802 A French balloonist made his second ascent in England (he landed in Chingford)

● 1844 A tribe of Red Indians from Iowa set up camp as part of the fiftieth anniversary celebrations at Lord's

● 1868 A team of Aborigines gave a demonstration of boomerang throwing

● 1874 A team of baseball players from Boston and Philadelphia gave a display of their sport

● 1914 Lord's was used as a military camp

Meanwhile, the Public Schools of England had decided that cricket was not only very manly but also extremely 'decent', and they made it a respectable sport that would represent the honourable code of behaviour of any Englishman. Some of the strongest links with countries in the British Empire were forged through teaching the natives how to play cricket. Unfortunately, as with many British inventions since, other countries have acquired a nasty habit of doing it better.

One of the first overseas tours was by an unofficial 'All-England' team to the USA and Canada in 1859. For some reason, the game didn't catch on over there. The MCC, meanwhile, desperate to be seen as the *official* England team, organized tours to Australia. In 1877, to everyone's surprise but the Australians', Australia won a match against the MCC. This was later to become known as the first Test match — a 'test' between the strength of two countries. By one of those typically eccentric cricket traditions, England was thereafter (until 1977) always called 'MCC' when it played abroad, except, of course, when it played a Test match, when it became England again. (Got it?)

The popularity of cricket brought about a Golden Age (which finished at the outset of World War I), when batsmen developed much more elegant strokeplay and bowlers learned that they could make the ball do all sorts of unpredictable things (like googlies). The modern game had arrived. Then, between the wars, along came Mr Bradman .

Who was this Bradman bloke?

In 1928, a young Australian called Don Bradman played his first match for Australia. Don Bradman was a good batsman. In fact he was a sensation, and, statistically, he remains head and shoulders above anyone else who has ever played cricket. Quite simply, hardly anybody could get him out, which meant that he usually batted for several hours, scoring vast numbers of runs in the process.

Because Bradman was so good, England (under a captain called Douglas Jardine) decided to try a new tactic in 1932. Rather than aiming to hit the stumps, they would aim to bounce the ball directly at Bradman's (and any other Australian's) body. The famous Bodyline series caused a huge diplomatic incident and led to a change in the Laws of cricket. But dangerous, intimidating bowling was in for good. (Or rather, for bad.)

Batsman fends off bodyline bowling while the <u>leg trap</u> fielders wait for the catch

Why do they complain that cricket isn't what it was?

There have been a lot of big changes to cricket since World War II. First, they removed the distinction between amateur and professional cricket. By 1962, even the amateurs were earning a bit on the side. The influence of the stuffy MCC on the game had been so strong until this time that the upper crust 'amateurs' would always get changed in different dressing rooms from their team-mates, the 'professionals'.

Soon afterwards, in a move to make cricket more exciting, a <u>limited overs</u> competition was started up by Gillette in 1963. Limited overs cricket (see p.95) became very popular because there were more incidents per hour, and because it was usually all over in a day. However, the old guard and traditionalists felt that one day cricket cheapened the values of the game, and removed much of its subtlety. (Which, to a large extent, is true.)

In 1977, about the time that Ian Botham was launching his career for England, a man called Kerry Packer defied the authorities by setting up an unofficial cricket circus in Australia. This involved all sorts of innovations like floodlit cricket, coloured clothing and lots of money for the players who joined it. Although the great rift was later healed, cricketers across the world were subsequently much more highly paid.

Which practically brings us up to the present day.

But it still begs one very important question...

3

What is Cricket?

Is it like rounders?

There is a game called rounders (the ancestor of American baseball) that you almost certainly played as a youngster. You remember how you would divide into two teams. The first team would get ready by scattering at random around the field in positions where they thought they would catch the ball (or where they hoped the ball would not come anywhere near them). One of this team would then be picked to be the ball-thrower. If the ball-thrower turned out to be no good, somebody else would have a turn.

Meanwhile, the second team would stand in a line and each player would take it in turns to hold the rounders bat and try to hit the ball as far as possible (and sometimes actually make contact). He or she would then go hurtling round the bases trying to score a complete rounder, but would rarely manage this because:

- the ball would go up in the air and mean old Uncle Tom would catch it; or
- the ball would get to the person standing on first base (usually marked by a pile of jumpers) before the batter did, and the batter would therefore be out. (In fact, this is called run out.)

When everyone in the batting team was out (the end of the innings), the two teams swapped over. And finally, when the

22

other team had all had a turn, you counted up how many rounders had been scored, and the team with the most rounders was the winner. Simple.

Well, the good news is that if you understand rounders then you understand the basics of cricket. Like rounders, cricket is played by two teams who take it in turns to be the fielding team and the batting team. Each player has a go at being a batter (except in cricket you must call him a batsman) until he is <u>out</u>. And, just as in rounders, the batsman can get caught out or run out, or a-lot-of-other-things-out. If he is out, it is the end of his turn (which is officially known as his innings – the same word that describes the whole team's performance).

Instead of scoring 'rounders', both teams try to score as many <u>runs</u> as possible, and the team with the most runs at the end is almost certainly the winner. At least, in cricket the team with the most runs is almost certainly not the loser. Look, I must be honest here and say that winning in cricket is a little more complicated than rounders, but you will have to wait until the chapter called 'Who's Winning?' to find out more.

However, comparing cricket with rounders is like comparing chess with draughts. Yes, chess and draughts are both played on a chequered board, and cricket and rounders are both played on

---

5 DIFFERENCES BETWEEN CRICKET AND BASEBALL

● Cricketers run in straight lines, not in circles

● No baseball fielder would be stupid enough to stand at silly mid off

● When did a baseball match last stop for afternoon tea?

● Baseball players always play in pyjamas (cricketers only sometimes)

● Cricketers sometimes wear baseball caps, but baseball players never wear cricket caps

---

a field: to the newly arrived Martian they do probably look the same. But cricket – like chess – is a considerably more subtle game than its counterpart. Which is where the rest of this book comes in...

How many people play in a cricket match?

Cricket is a game played by two teams, each with eleven players. Well, the convention is to have eleven players. If the captains agree beforehand, there is nothing to stop a game of cricket having twenty people in each team, or twenty in one team and eleven in the other. This used to happen back in Ye Olde Days of cricket (in 1826, say). Nowadays, with so much money in the game, no club can afford to pay twenty men to stand out in a field all day even if it wants to.

So eleven players it always is. (Except that on cold, windy Saturdays in April my team is doing well to scrape together ten.)

What happens on the cricket field?

The cynical observer of a cricket match would say: 'nothing happens on the cricket field'. In reality, of course, there are always lots of things happening on the cricket field. It's just that some of them are in the players' minds, so you can't necessarily see them.

Before they start, the two captains toss a coin. One of the teams becomes the batting team and the other team becomes the fielding team – just like in rounders. Then the game begins.

If you look out at the cricket field during a match there should always be fifteen people out there. Eleven of these are the fielding team. Two of them are batsmen (there are always two batsmen in at any one time). And the two men in white coats are not from the local asylum but are in fact umpires, there to apply the Laws.

One of the batsmen (the striker) stands ready to receive a ball from the bowler while the other (the non striker) waits next to the umpire at the opposite end of the pitch. The bowler now runs up and bowls the ball.

One of several things might now happen. The batsman might hit the ball, leave the ball, miss the ball; then start running, stand still or give out a groan and start walking back towards the

striker

wicket-keeper

batting crease

PITCH

off side

leg side

bowler

non striker

umpire

pavilion. If the last of these happens, it probably means he is out. More about this in a moment.

What the batsman is hoping to do is to score runs, which he does by hitting the ball and running to the other end of the pitch. More – much more – about this later on. However, he is also trying not to get out, so he doesn't want to take too many risks. Unlike in rounders, he is under no obligation to hit the ball every time, so in fact he may hang around for quite a while just leaving the ball and getting used to the conditions. This is called getting his eye in. It gives the crowd the opportunity to have a chat.

The main thing that the bowler is trying to do out there is get rid of one of the batsmen by getting him out. He can do this in many ways, the most spectacular being when he knocks over the stumps that are behind the batsman. If the batsman is out, that is the end of his innings and he walks off to be replaced by the next man in the team. The bowler will generally be trying to bowl straight at the stumps, but because he is stiff, his first few balls (known as looseners) may be a bit erratic. This gives the crowd more opportunity for a chat.

The bowlers take it in turns to try to get the batsmen out. The first bowler, having decided with the captain which end he wants to bowl from, will mark his run up and then bowl at the batsman. He will go through this little routine six times.

Why do they all change ends?

At the end of a bowler's sequence of six balls (known as an over), the umpire shouts 'Over!' (that's why). If no runs have been scored in the over, it is called a maiden over, presumably be-cause it is pure and untouched.

The fielders now change ends (and the batsmen stay where they are). If you watch cricket on television, you may be fooled into thinking that they don't change ends at all. This is because the BBC always has a camera at both ends, and at the end of the over, the producer magically flicks from Camera One to Camera Two. So on telly you always get to see cricket from the bowler's point of view. ('Disgusted' from Tunbridge Wells would prefer to see it from the batsman's point of view, however.)

Once they have done this end-changing, a different bowler then comes in to bowl his six balls. The reason why the fielders change ends like this has been lost in the mists of time, but it means that:

- both of the batsmen who are <u>in</u> will have a roughly equal share of receiving the ball;
- because both ends of the pitch are used, the pitch lasts for twice as much time before it gets worn out (thus saving the groundsman some work);
- if there is a down-wind, the bowling side benefit from it as much as they suffer from it at the other end, while the sun will only be in the batsman's eyes for half of the time;
- the spectators get to see the game from two different perspectives without having to move.

All of this frantic activity keeps on going, with batsmen batting and running, bowlers bowling, and fielders fielding and changing ends, until ten of the batsmen are out, or until something else intervenes (like lunch, rain or the discovery that one of the teams has won).

Yes, but what's the point of it all?

Well, at its very crudest, the purpose of cricket is for the batting team to score as many runs as possible, and for the bowling team to finish the batting team's innings as quickly as possible by bowl-

---

5 QUOTES ON CRICKET

- 'Cricket is organized loafing.' – William Temple, Archbishop of Canterbury

- 'Cricket is baseball on Valium.' – Robin Williams

- 'Basically it's just a whole bunch of blokes standing around scratching themselves.' – Kathy Lette

- 'Cricket is not so much a game as a substitute religion. It certainly gives one a very clear idea of eternity.' – Lord St John of Fawsley

- 'If there is cricket in heaven, let us also pray that there will be rain.' – Arthur Marshall

ing out the batsmen. Of course, cricket is also about many other things, like having a nice tea on a sunny afternoon, but we'll stick to the technical bits for the moment.

Although one of the aims of cricket is undoubtedly for the participants to try to win, this isn't necessarily as important as you might think. You see, although it is a team game, another of the purposes of cricket is to enable individuals to do something heroic (regardless of whether their team wins or not). So while each batsman is trying to score as many runs as possible which count towards the team's <u>total</u> score, he is also desperately concerned about his own personal score. Similarly, while each bowler is trying to get out the batsmen so that his team can win, he is also looking to build up his personal tally of wickets.

A batsman who scores a <u>century</u> (one hundred runs) is treated as a hero, and is rightly greeted with a standing ovation. Bowlers who take five wickets in an innings are also heroes. Even the old buffer in village cricket has a chance to be a hero, if he takes an unexpected catch or scores the winning run.

Scoring a century or a fifty (the latter is any innings of between fifty and ninety-nine runs) is seen as passing a landmark. Scoring forty-nine runs and then being out is regarded as something of a failure and also as a blatant attempt to avoid buying drinks for your colleagues after the match. Worst of all, though, is scoring no runs at all. This is called a <u>duck</u>, apparently because the number nought is the shape of a duck's egg. (Likewise, in tennis nought is called love, which comes from *l'oeuf*, which is a French egg. Not a lot of people know that.)

As well as wanting to be heroic, a batsman likes to bat for as long as possible because it gives him something interesting to do. Likewise, unless he is either exhausted or his bowling is being hit around the ground by the batsmen, a bowler is always keen to bowl as much as possible: it keeps him involved at the very heart of the game. If he isn't bowling, he may be sent to a remote corner of the field to rest, pick his fingernails, and throw the ball back if it comes to him (which will be about once every ten minutes).

How are runs scored?

A batsman scores one run by hitting the ball and running to the other end of the pitch, known as the non striker's end. (Meanwhile, his partner crosses over with him to the striker's end, and thus becomes the striker). If the batsman runs to the other end of the pitch and back again, he gets two runs, and in theory if he were to run the length of the pitch ten times, he would get ten runs. The reason why this rarely happens is that if the ball crosses the line, rope, hedge or ditch around the ground (known as the boundary) the batsman automatically gets four runs, or six if it crosses the boundary without bouncing. Legend

---

5 UNUSUAL CRICKET MATCHES

- 1735 Two teams in Bromley played a game of cricket on horseback

- 1796 A team of one-legged Greenwich pensioners beat a team of one-armed Greenwich pensioners by 103 runs

- 1823 The crews of the ships *Hecla* and *Fury* played a game at Igooli in Antarctica

- 1838 In Manchester, eleven 'first choice' cricketers beat eleven men and a catapult

- 1931 At Knockholt, a team of players all called Smithers beat a team who were all named Streatfield

---

does, however, tell of a ball going down a rabbit hole and the batsmen scoring forty runs before the ball was retrieved.

Very occasionally the fielder throws the ball back and the player standing next to the stumps fails to stop it. The batsmen are allowed to keep running if this happens, and such runs are known as overthrows. I once saw a batsman – Alan Knott in a Test match against the West Indies – score seven runs off one ball this way, thanks to two bad throws. This is the sort of obscure cricketing incident that the cricket fan likes to recount to his grandchildren, before the grandchildren make their excuses and run outside to play.

Runs can also be scored without the batsman hitting the ball. Such runs are called extras or, in Australia, sundries. Extras are not counted towards the batsman, but do sometimes count against the bowler, and always count towards the team's total of runs.

The four types of extra are:

- **Wide** If the ball is bowled so that the batsman misses it, and indeed could not have reached it without doing himself a nasty injury, this is known as a wide. One run is added to extras.

wide

- **No ball** If the bowler's front foot goes beyond the bowling crease, or if the bowler does anything else grossly illegal, the

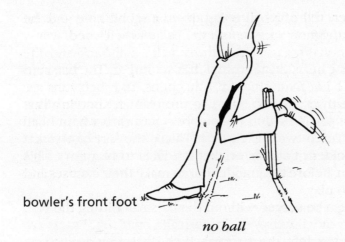

bowler's front foot

no ball

umpire shouts 'no ball'. If the batsman hits the no ball and runs, the runs are added to his total as normal. If the batsman doesn't hit runs off a no ball, Mr Extras is given one run instead.

- Leg byes If the ball hits the batsman's leg (or anything else other than his bat, glove or helmet) he can run to the other end, and extras is credited with one leg bye. To get a leg bye, however, the batsman has to have been attempting to hit the ball or actively trying (and failing) to avoid being hit.

- Byes If the ball misses the bat and everything else, and the wicket-keeper fails to stop it, the batsmen can run a bye.

When an extra happens, the umpire makes an elaborate arm signal to inform the scorer. The signals used are shown on page 76. A no ball or a wide means that the ball doesn't count towards the six ball over – and also, when the statistics of the game are published, the run is counted against the bowler, which is why he usually looks annoyed when he sees the signal.

Suppose a cricket match started about an hour ago. This is what the score might look like now:

Snipcock: not out	25
Tweed: not out	20
Extras: (1b 4, nb 2)	6
TOTAL:	51 for no wicket

Hurriedly swallowing his piece of chocolate cake, the radio commentator would describe this by saying: 'and the batsmen have just reached the fifty partnership – the score is fifty-one for no wicket, with Snipcock twenty-five not out and Tweed twenty not out'.

What this means is that Snipcock has scored twenty-five runs so far, Tweed has made twenty, and there have been six extras (four leg byes, two no balls) so the team has scored fifty-one runs. The partnership is the number of runs that have been scored since the last wicket fell: in fact there hasn't been a wicket yet – both of the opening batsmen are still not out. (They have done well!)

How do you get somebody out?

There are eleven different ways in which a batsman can be out. For most of these the bowler gets the credit. Not that the batsman really cares who gets the credit – all that matters to him is that he is out, and he may have nothing interesting to do for the rest of the day. (Meanwhile, the other batsman stays in, ready to start a new partnership with the next batsman.)

The most common ways of getting out (roughly in order of how often they happen) are as follows:

● Caught Just as in rounders, if the batsman hits the ball with his bat, or his glove holding the bat, and the ball is caught by any of the fielding team before it bounces, the batsman is out caught. The only exceptions to this are if the ball was deemed by the umpire to be a 'no ball' (see p.30), or if the fielder catches the ball outside the boundary, or deliberately uses an artificial aid (like his cap or a deck chair) to catch the ball. In this last case, a penalty of five runs is awarded to the batsman.

If the bowler is very fast, or the ball is swerving in the air (swinging) or deviating at strange angles off the pitch, the batsman is quite likely to hit the ball on the edge of his bat. This is why you often see several men in a line behind the wicket. These are called the slips, and they have two duties: to catch the ball, and to give the wicket-keeper somebody to talk to.

● Bowled If the batsman misses the ball and it hits the stumps behind him, he is out bowled. If the ball hits the bat or the pad, or hits anything else on the batsman before hitting the stumps, this is also out bowled. This can sometimes be very

32

bowled

spectacular (one of the stumps may be knocked flying), but you are just as much out if the ball grazes the top of the stumps and knocks off one of those little pieces of wood on top of the stumps, known as <u>bails</u>. If by some miracle (and it has happened) the ball hits the stumps and both of the bails stay balanced on top, the batsman is not out.

In general, bad batsmen are bowled more often than good batsmen. This is because good batsmen usually know how to get *something* in the way. However, this may lead to…

LBW One of the most baffling forms of <u>dismissal</u> is LBW which stands for <u>leg before wicket</u>. Even many cricketers don't understand exactly how it works. LBW happens when the batsman misses the ball and it hits some part of his anatomy – and was otherwise going on to hit the stumps. Actually it's a little more complicated than this – the diagram on page 34 explains it better.

The reason for having LBW is to stop batsmen from just blocking the ball with their bodies. This would make cricket very tedious even to those people who generally find it interesting.

Whether a batsman is LBW or not is entirely in the judgement of the umpire – which is why it is usually so controver-

LBW

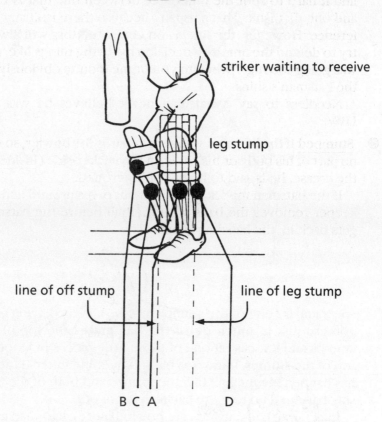

striker waiting to receive

leg stump

line of off stump

line of leg stump

B C A   D

Here are four situations where the batsman has missed the ball and the ball has hit his body. For each one the umpire has to decide if the batsman is out LBW.

(WARNING: WHAT FOLLOWS SHOULD NOT BE READ BY ANYONE WITH A WEAK HEART)

A – *This is definitely out LBW. The ball would have hit the stumps, and hit the batsman in line with the stumps.*

B – *This is definitely not out. The ball was never going to hit the stumps.*

C – *A bit more complicated: the ball would have hit the stumps, but hit the batsman outside the line of off stump. This is only out LBW if the batsman did not attempt to hit the ball with his bat.*

D – *Here is the final twist: you can't be out LBW if the ball bounces outside the line of leg stump. So, although this looks the same as A, it is in fact not out…*

sial. If you see the ball hit the batsman's <u>pads</u> on TV, you may find it hard to spot the difference between one that *is* LBW and one that isn't. That's usually because there isn't any difference. However, the television commentators will always try to defend the umpire's decision by saying things like 'that was going too high' when to you or me it quite obviously hit the batsman's shins.

Needless to say, a batsman never believes he was out LBW.

<u>Stumped</u> If the batsman wanders towards the bowler, so that no part of his body or his bat is on the wicket-side (<u>inside</u>) of the crease, he is said to be out of his <u>ground</u>.

If the batsman misses the ball, is out of his ground and the keeper removes the bails with the ball before the batsman gets back <u>in</u>, the batsman is out...

stumped

The threat of being stumped is what stops a batsman from <u>dancing</u> down the pitch and taking a great heave at the ball – although you will sometimes see this happen.

run out

🏏 <u>Run out</u> If the batsman is out of his ground and is trying to score a run, 'stumped' becomes 'run out' — another rounders-like dismissal. Either batsman can be run out at either end, by any of the fielders.

Run outs are usually the fault of the batsman who first <u>called</u> 'Yes' to run when it turns out a run wasn't possible. It is the batsman who ends up nearest to the wicket which the ball hits who is out.

There is only one greater tragedy in cricket than the caller being run out, and that is the non-caller being run out. (What could be worse than being out when it wasn't even your fault?) It usually takes several years for a batsman to forgive his partner for running him out.

🏏 <u>Hit wicket</u> The batsman is out if he accidentally knocks over his stumps with his bat. This usually happens when the batsman loses his balance while trying a particularly extravagant swish shot (that's not a technical term, by the way). However, if the batsman's hat or toupee is blown off as the ball approaches him, and goes on to knock one of the bails off, that is also out.

hit wicket

Those are all the main ways of being out. But the batsman can also be out for such crimes as picking up the ball without permission (handling the ball), obstructing the field, hitting the ball twice, failing to come on to the field quickly enough (timed out), or being told to retire by his captain so that a new batsman can have a go.

obstructing the field

If a batsman does not succumb to any of these dismissals before the end of the innings, he is not out. (A broken finger or a bout of Delhi belly may result in <u>retired hurt</u> which counts as not out, too.) Being not out is a good thing – good for the ego because it means that you were 'undefeated', and more importantly good for the batting <u>average</u>, the statistic on which batsmen are most commonly judged. (The batting average is calculated by dividing the number of runs a batsman has scored in the season by the number of times that he has been out.)

In all the most common dismissals except for run out, the credit of the wicket is given to the bowler. Thus a bowler can get a wicket for his own skilful bowling or for the misjudgement (or ineptitude) of the batsman, or for the brilliant catching of the fielder. Sometimes all three. In most (but not all!) statistics he gets just as much credit for dismissing a good batsman as for dismissing someone who can't bat. The most common statistic on which the bowler is judged is the bowling average: this is the number of runs the bowler has conceded in the season, divided by the number of wickets he has taken.

Very occasionally you see a bowler take a wicket only to discover that the umpire has shouted 'no ball'. This is another of cricket's tragedies, since the bowler can only blame himself. A no ball means that the batsman cannot be out caught, bowled, LBW, stumped or hit wicket.

When, and why, do they all shout 'Howzat!'?

If the ball knocks over the batsman's stumps, it is obvious to all concerned that he is out. However, in other circumstances it is less obvious – in which case the bowler and/or a fielder has to <u>appeal</u> to the umpire, who then makes his decision. An appeal has to be made in the correct manner, which is to ask the umpire, 'How was that?' In the excitement of the moment, this normally sounds more like 'Howzat!' or even 'OWAZAAATT!!!', both of which are acceptable. However, if you were to politely turn to the umpire and say, 'My dear man, I think that may be out – what do you say?' he would give you a scornful look and ask you to appeal properly.

If the umpire thinks that it is out, he raises his index finger in front of him. (Lest there be any confusion, no other finger or thumb will do.)

The most common occasions when the umpire has to answer an appeal are:

- for an LBW;
- for a catch off the <u>edge</u> of the bat, if it is unclear whether the faint sound was that of ball on bat, ball on pad or bat on pad;
- for run out or stumped.

In the good old days, if a batsman knew he was out, he <u>walked</u> without waiting for the umpire – a truly sportsmanlike gesture. These days, even in village cricket, a batsman who has quite patently edged the ball may wait for a decision because there is always a chance that the umpire may not have noticed (or, shame on him, that the umpire may in some way be biased in the batsman's favour). In the old sense of the expression, this is 'not cricket'.

And finally, if you ever hear a television commentator analysing an action replay of an LBW appeal and saying 'that was definitely worth a <u>shout</u>' you can be almost certain that he thinks it was out.

All of which probably sounds unfair, amusing, arbitrary and even eccentric. Perhaps you are beginning to get the picture now.

ONE INNINGS FROM A REAL MATCH

England v Australia, Perth 1979

Australia – 2nd innings

Wiener	c Randall	b Underwood	58
Laird	c Taylor	b Underwood	33
Border	c Taylor	b Willis	115
Chappell G.	st Taylor	b Underwood	43
Hughes	c Miller	b Botham	4
Toohey	c Taylor	b Botham	3
Marsh	c Gower	b Botham	4
Bright	lbw	b Botham	12
Lillee	c Willey	b Dilley	19
Dymock	not out		20
Thomson		b Botham	8
Extras	(b 4, lb 5, nb 7, w 2)		18
TOTAL			337

Fall of wickets: 91-1, 100-2, 168-3, 183-4, 191-5, 204-6, 225-7, 303-8, 323-9, 337-10

	O(vers)	M(aidens)	R(uns)	W(ickets)
Bowling: Dilley	18	3	50	1
Botham	45.5	14	98	5
Willis	26	7	52	1
Underwood	41	14	82	3
Miller	10	0	36	0
Willey	1	0	1	0

Things to notice:

● *Seven of Australia's batsmen were out caught, but Chappell was stumped, Bright was lbw and Thomson was bowled.*

● *The partnership between Wiener and Laird for the first wicket was 91 runs (commentators would call this a solid start to the innings).*

● *Botham bowled more than anyone else, he conceded 98 runs, but also took 5 wickets in the innings, including the last one (which is why he didn't finish his 46th over – 45.5 means 45 overs and 5 balls).*

● *Lillee was out caught Willey bowled Dilley, a freak coincidence of names which has ensured that this match will never be forgotten.*

4
Who's Winning?

If there is one thing you should avoid at all costs when watching a cricket match, it is asking the question 'Who's winning?' As far as a cricketer is concerned, a match is not won or lost until the very last ball is bowled, simply because, even if a side has only one more run to score with no batsmen out, total disaster is still possible. Asking 'Who's winning' is tantamount to saying, 'I know absolutely nothing about the subtleties of the game of cricket, please ignore me from now on.' Even when it seems a perfectly legitimate question to ask, don't ask it.

Who's winning?

What you might ask is 'Which side is on top?' to which the answer may be 'England' (occasionally) or 'West Indies', 'Australia' etc (more often). One of the charms of cricket – one of the reasons why you may one day become addicted to it – is that, more than in any other sport, the situation in a match can change drastically in the space of a couple of minutes. One side can be well on top, then one of the batsmen is out. Suddenly what seemed to be a relaxed game in which the batsmen had no problem tonking the ball all over the place, becomes nail-bitingly tense. The crowd buzzes (if there is a crowd). The fielders look sharper and probably move into more attacking positions (they come closer to the batsman). As a result the batsmen suddenly look and act worried.

How do you win at cricket?

Before I answer this question, you need to know that there are three types of cricket match:

- one innings matches (the type usually played on village greens on Saturday afternoons, in which each team bats only once);

- two innings matches (usually first class cricket, played by counties, states and countries, in which the teams are allowed to bat twice);

---

5 CRICKETING KNIGHTS

- Sir Len Hutton (England)

- Sir Garfield Sobers (West Indies)

- Sir Donald Bradman (Australia)

- Sir Richard Hadlee (New Zealand)

- Sir Charles Aubrey Smith (England, then Hollywood)

42

● limited overs matches (in which each team bats once for a fixed number of overs, sometimes wearing garishly coloured clothing, while the crowd gets very drunk).

These types of cricket are described in more detail in the chapter called 'Do Cricket Matches Last For Ever?' The way you win each type differs slightly, but in essence, there are always two requirements for winning a match. A team wins if:

● it scores more runs than the other team; and (except for limited overs)

● the batsmen in the other team are either <u>all out</u>, or the captain of the opposing team has <u>declared</u> (see below) his final innings finished before all his team have batted.

'All out' is when ten of the eleven batsmen are out. There is always one 'not out' batsman at the end of an innings – the rule being that you aren't allowed to bat in cricket if there is no batsman at the other end. Amongst other things it would be very lonely.

Winning a one innings match

By far the most simple version of cricket is the one innings match. Here is an example:

Little Snoring 210 for 3 declared
Great Snoring 155 all out

Little Snoring wins by 55 runs.

Here is another:

Great Snoring 160 for 8 declared
Little Snoring 161 for 7

Little Snoring has three wickets left when it overtakes Great Snoring's score, and so wins by three wickets. (Little Snoring does not continue batting when it has overtaken Great Snoring – that's the end of the match.)

You will see that in both of these village matches, the first team declared. This often happens. Declaring is when the captain decides to finish his team's innings before everyone has batted (see also 'What About Tactics?'). The captain will only usually declare if:

● his team batted first; and

● he believes that his team has scored enough runs to win without all of his players having to bat.

Little Snoring's declaration in the first match was successful because they won. Great Snoring's in the second was less so because they lost (but then maybe it was a good game, and in cricket that's often all that matters).

If the captain declares for any other reason, he is either insane or has a particular reason for wanting to finish the match early (so that he can get home to host a dinner party, for example).

Very occasionally, this happens:

Great Snoring 150 for 5 declared
Little Snoring 150 all out

This rare and exciting result is known as a tie. It is a tie because the teams finished with the same score and the second team were all out. A tie is *not* the same as a draw. If you want to find out about draws, skip the next section…

Winning a two innings match

In a two innings match each team has two innings if there is time (and if it is necessary). In order to win a two innings match, the conditions stated earlier still apply, but the winners have to bowl out the opponents twice. The side that wins, however, does not always have to bat twice – it is possible that the winning side scores more runs in one innings than the opponents do in two. Here is a real example of such a match:

(England v West Indies, Old Trafford, 1988)
England first innings   135 all out
West Indies first innings   384 for 7 declared
England second innings   93 all out
West Indies second innings   Didn't happen (because it wasn't necessary)

West Indies bowled out England twice for a total of 228 runs – 156 runs fewer than the West Indies' first innings' score. West Indies therefore won by an innings and 156 runs. (The British

44

press, however, prefers its headlines to be about England, so it would have described this result as 'England lose by an innings and 156 runs', together with shock-horror words like SHAMBLES! and DISGRACE!). Losing by an innings, as you might have gathered, is the nice way of saying ignominious defeat.

There is one other technicality that you should at least be aware of: if the team that bats first scores a lot of runs, and the team that bats second scores considerably fewer, then the first team may be able to ask the other team to play their second innings straight after their first.* This is a tactic. It is known as enforcing the follow-on.

How can you spend five days playing cricket and still draw?

Despite the best intentions of the captains at the beginning of the match, games of cricket often finish as draws. (Except for limited overs cricket, which always ends with one side winning – more of which on p.95). One of the concepts non-cricketers find most difficult to grasp is that a draw is a very common, and quite acceptable, result in most forms of cricket – even if the match lasts for five days.

Throughout a cricket match, the captain is looking to make attacking moves which will help his side to win, whilst at the same time making defensive moves that will prevent his side from losing (a bit like in chess). It is these tactics that make cricket such an interesting game to many people (if not everyone) and an introduction to these tactics is given in a later chapter. However, it is also this element of cat and mouse that can lead to a match ending as a draw (like a chess player's stalemate).

Draws can actually be quite exciting – on many occasions there have been nine wickets down, with the last two batsmen in and only a few runs still to get for victory before time ran out.

In a famous and stirring poem by Sir Henry Newbolt, which brings tears to many a cricket-lover's eyes, one verse starts:

> 'There's a breathless hush in the close to-night
> Ten to make and the match to win
> A bumping pitch and a blinding light
> An hour to play and the last man in…'

*In a Test match the difference between the first innings' scores would have to be more than 200 runs before this could happen.

The poem does not reveal the result of this match, but it is just possible that it ended in a draw. With a whole hour left to play and only ten more runs needed for victory (or one more wicket for defeat) I would agree that this is unlikely – but stranger things have happened in cricket.

There are, however, matches which are not so breathlessly hushed: well before the finish they can reach a position from which it is obvious that neither side is going to win. Both captains finally realize that the game is heading nowhere and the match peters out.

Here is an example of a dull draw in a one innings match:

Little Snoring   195 all out
Much Grinding 135 for 5

The reason why this game was drawn is because it ran out of time before Much Grinding had overtaken Little Snoring, and before Much Grinding were all out. (In this case, the agreed finish time for the match was seven o'clock, which just happened to coincide with the opening time of the Snoring Arms.) A lot of games end up as draws. This includes about half of all international Test matches, despite the fact that they last for five days.

One of the main factors behind this is the weather...

---

5 OCCASIONS WHEN THE ENGLISH WEATHER HAS STOPPED PLAY

- 1868 Excessive heat stopped play between Surrey and Lancashire

- 1946 Fog stopped play between Glamorgan and Hampshire

- 1963 Dazzling sunlight (reflecting off car windscreens) stopped play between Essex and Derbyshire

- 1975 (June) Snow stopped play between Derbyshire and Lancashire

- 1981 Cold stopped play between Cambridge University and Essex

---

Why is it always raining?

Perhaps the most common reason for matches being drawn is the weather. A frustration shared by players and spectators alike (especially in England) is the threat of rain.

As you've probably noticed, cricket is more sensitive to rain than most other sports. In football or rugby, the players play in almost all weather, part of the fun being returning to the dressing room completely covered in mud. In professional cricket, however, the slightest hint of a rain shower and the players immediately leave the field. You may think this sounds a bit soft, but there are very good reasons for it:

● rain affects the pitch, which may give the bowling side an unfair advantage. At the sight of rain, the groundsmen therefore hurtle out with the <u>covers</u>.

● a wet <u>outfield</u> damages the ball, and the slippery surface is a danger to the knees of the bowlers. (By the age of thirty, most <u>fast bowlers</u> have knees that are held together by piano wire.)

It is also widely suspected that the players are often rather anxious to finish the game of poker they began earlier in the day back in the pavilion.

Of course when cricketers want to play in the rain, they do. Village matches quite often continue for hours in steady drizzle.

Bad light

Bad light is another hazard. If you watch a professional match in overcast weather, you will see the two umpires regularly checking the level on their light meters. When the light reaches a certain dimness (a level is agreed before the match), the umpires offer the light to the batsmen. They should only do this if the batsmen are in physical danger from one or more of the bowlers, but sometimes the light is offered when there are slow bowlers bowling. This is a source of immense annoyance to spectators, especially since, when offered the light, the batsmen nearly always accept and leave the field. (This leads many cricket spectators to question whether the players want to be playing at all.)

The real frustration is that once professional cricketers have left the field, they and the umpires seem very reluctant to come back on again. One of cricket's more absurd rituals has been established in recent years whereby:

- the umpires come on to the field without their white coats and prod the field gingerly;

- having decided it is all right to resume play, the umpires announce that play will begin in twenty minutes (presumably so they can put their coats on);

- the umpires eventually come back on, to ironic cheers, followed about five minutes later by a straggling bunch of players.

All of this slows down play. All of it helps to draw matches.

5

What Do All the People Do?

All of the eleven players in the team have to bat, regardless of their ability. They are all allowed to bowl, too. In practice, when selecting a team the selectors will always try to pick a balanced side, made up of:

- six reliable batsmen;

- five reliable bowlers (usually different types of bowler, to give the captain options – see sections on 'Tactics' and 'Bowlers');

- a *specialist* wicket-keeper (preferably a reasonable batsman, too).

You will notice that this adds up to twelve. Since it is supposed to add up to eleven, if the captain is lucky one of the batsmen is also a good bowler (or vice versa). Such a player is called an all-rounder. The most famous of recent times has been Ian Botham – who was, in his prime, England's most devastating bowler and exciting batsman. He is a great fielder, too.

As a spectator, there is interest to be had in watching batsmen, bowlers, fielders and umpires. In the next few pages, we look at some of the things you should be watching for.

Batsmen

What is the batting order?

The eleven players go out to bat in what is called the batting

Ian Botham, England Superhero

order. This batting order is usually fixed by the captain before the match, although he is allowed to change the order at any time if he wants to.

It is usual to get your best six batsman to be the first six in the batting order. This is because:

- batting is harder when the bowlers are fresh and the ball is new;

- a good batsman can bat for a long time, and all that stops him from going on for days is that either he is out, or he runs out of partners at the other end;

- the good batsmen are pretty miffed if they don't get a decent chance to bat.

Batsmen come in all shapes, sizes and styles. Some spectators prefer the gritty ones with solid technique who may score slowly but are great to have in a crisis. Geoff Boycott of Yorkshire and England was a very famous example. Others prefer the attacking, aggressive batsmen who hit sixes (often lots of them). Viv Richards of the West Indies has been one of the most famous of recent times.

Finally there are the artists, those who delight the crowd with the elegance of their strokeplay. It is something of a comment on English cricket that in the last twenty years, the only such player whose name has been on everyone's lips is David Gower. Gower's batting is so laid-back it is practically horizontal. (Metaphorically speaking, that is – nobody bats horizontally!).

Other countries seem to have produced a lot more of these classic batsmen in the last decade: twin brothers Steve and Mark Waugh of Australia, Dilip Vengsarkar of India, Martin Crowe of New Zealand and Jeffrey Dujon of the West Indies would all (in my opinion) come into this category. Classic batsmen don't necessarily score more runs, but they do make the crowd go 'Oooh'.

When does the best batsman bat?

I'm sorry to duck the issue, but the answer depends on what you mean by 'best'. If you are judging by who tends to score the most runs (and has the highest average or world rating), the 'best' and most exciting batsman usually bats at number four or five. This is because he comes in when the bowlers are a little tired and he can launch the offensive – the rate of scoring usually increases as the innings progresses after a solid foundation by the openers.

However there are many exceptions. One of England's best batsmen of recent years, Graham Gooch, bats at number one. Ian Botham has batted at number six or seven for England.

All things being equal, though, the well balanced batting order will look something like this:

Position

1 & 2	The opening batsmen or openers
3, 4 & 5	The strokeplayers (usually more exciting than openers)
6	The all-rounder
7	The wicket-keeper who can bat reasonably well

The best batsman… …and the rabbit

8 & 9	Know how to hold the bat properly
10	Knows how to waft a bat at the ball
11	If he lasts more than five balls, he is doing well

Nine, ten and eleven are known as the tailenders. Numbers ten and eleven are often known as rabbits, because they don't hang around for very long. Certain international teams in recent years (who will remain nameless) seem to have had rabbits from number four downwards.

You might expect the first six batsmen to average about forty runs per innings, and numbers seven to eleven to average between twenty-five and five as you move down the order.

It often helps to have one or two left-handers in the team (David Gower, Allan Border and Neil Fairbrother being famous examples). Left-handed batsmen stand the other way round, so that the bowler has to adjust the direction he is aiming the ball in. This can disrupt the rhythm of the bowlers, which means they will bowl bad balls, which means the batsman can hit lots of runs. That, at least, is the theory.

Why do batsmen tap the ground with their bats?

Cricket is a game of rituals, many of which are to do with batting. The first ritual happens when a <u>new batsman</u> comes in: all the fielders will clap him (in friendly cricket, at least).

You will then see him hold his bat vertically and call to (or gesticulate at) the umpire at the bowler's end. He is making sure that he is standing in exactly the right position (precise to a couple of millimetres) between the bowler and the stumps, so he can defend his wicket. The process of fixing position is known as <u>taking guard</u>. Most batsmen hold their bats in a line between <u>middle and leg</u> stumps, the hand signal for which happens to be a V sign.

The batsman will then mark the guard (sometimes with a long ritual of scraping and patting the ground) before looking around at where the fielders are placed. Most of this ritual is done to relax the nerves and to prolong a stay that may only last one ball.

The batsman is now ready to face the bowling. His natural <u>stance</u> may involve standing upright with his bat held horizontally behind him (baseball style), or bent over with his bat gently tapping the ground, or a frenzied oscillation between these two positions. The classic textbooks say that it is better to hold the bat down than up, but this theory seems to have been ignored by most English batsmen of modern times.

---

5 LITERARY CRICKET FANATICS

- Arthur Conan Doyle (played first class cricket)

- P G Wodehouse

- Harold Pinter

- Samuel Beckett (only first class cricketer to get a Nobel Prize)

- Stephen Fry

What is a square cut?

Apart from the way that he stands, the other thing that makes each batsman unique is the way he hits the ball. This is called his strokeplay. Unlike baseball, where each batter has only a limited number of ways and directions in which to hit the ball, the crick-

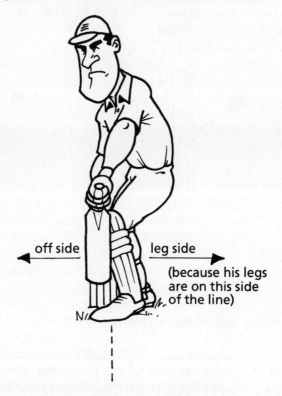

off side ◄

leg side ►

(because his legs
are on this side
of the line)

eter has all 360 degrees to play with. Some batsmen are good at hitting towards the off side while others are better on the leg side (otherwise called the on side).

The stroke that the batsman plays depends on what type of bowler is bowling, and also on where the ball bounces. There are two main types of shot that a batsman can play:

- if the ball bounces short (at least six feet in front of the batsman) he plays with his weight on the back foot (for example a square cut, or a backward defensive);

- if the ball bounces close to him (pitched up), he is more likely to lean forward to play off the front foot (for example a cover drive or a forward defensive).

These types of shot are the most common <u>textbook shots</u> that young boys would be taught at school. (This assumes that it is a school which teaches cricket: such schools are unfortunately on the decline, partly because of the pressures on teachers to do other things on Wednesday afternoons and Saturday mornings. I can't think what could be more important than cricket on a Wednesday afternoon or a Saturday morning, but there we are.) Some textbook shots are illustrated on page 56.

Of all of the <u>attacking shots</u> that exist (i.e. shots intended to score runs), many people find the cover drive the most elegant. The square cut is probably the most savage. The <u>hook</u> is the most courageous and risky (because of the risk of decapitation). The <u>late cut</u> – like a square cut but aimed in the direction of <u>first slip</u> – is certainly the most delicate (it always brings an appreciative rumble from a crowd). There is also a modern, unorthodox and extremely risky shot called a <u>reverse sweep</u>, which involves some very unnatural contortions on the batsman's part. The reverse sweep is frowned upon by all cricket textbooks.

square cut

backward
defensive

hook

forward
defensive

sweep

cover drive

Don't the batsmen get hurt?

As you may have observed, a cricket ball is hard. For this reason, batting can be quite dangerous. The natural human instinct to avoid pain usually comes into its own when batting, and the batsman knows how to avoid being hit. However, just in case, a batsman will always wear (leg) pads, gloves (which resemble a bunch of bananas) and what is known as a <u>box</u>, which protects his most sensitive region.

If very fast bowlers are around, the batsman will probably also wear a thigh pad, a chest pad and an arm guard. Even with these, he will often end up badly bruised.

Surprisingly, helmets only began to appear for the first time in 1980 – after which everyone realized what a good idea they were. In the old days, being felled by a bouncer was regarded as a manly way of collecting another battle scar. These days it means the loss of weeks of good income.

Bowlers

Who are the bowlers?

Everyone in the team has to bat at some time or other, but although everyone is allowed to bowl it is only rarely that this happens. In fact a captain will usually rely on just four men to bowl most if not all of the overs.

There are three types of bowler:

- fast bowlers (who take long, and sometimes ludicrously long, run ups);

- medium pacers (who typically take ten to twelve strides, sometimes known as seam bowlers or swing bowlers depending on their particular speciality);

- slow bowlers (who take very short run-ups and are usually spin bowlers, or spinners).

A bowler is not allowed to bowl an over from one end and then (after the fielders have changed ends) bowl the next over. This means that there are always two bowlers operating in tandem – one from the 'Pavilion End', as it might be called, the other from the 'City End', say. (The ends of pitches are always named after a local landmark or road to be found at that end of the ground.) This way the bowler gets a rest, usually standing in a fielding position that doesn't require too much running about, while his colleague bowls from the other end.

Eventually, though, a bowler does get tired, and the captain brings on somebody else. (Alternatively, the captain may take off a bowler because he is bowling badly!) If a bowler has been bowling a series of overs from one end without a break, this is called a spell. A bowler may have several spells in one day.

Why do bowlers have to make the ball bounce?

In baseball and rounders the ball doesn't bounce before you hit it, but in cricket the bowler always aims to bounce it. This is because it is much harder for a batsman to hit a bouncing ball than one that comes straight to him without bouncing – especially if he is playing on the sort of uneven pitch to be found in most villages. Also, if a cricket ball bounces, it can deviate in all sorts of directions, as you will discover shortly. In fact, the pitch is one of the most important things in cricket. A pitch can be easy or difficult to play on, it can be fast or slow, it can be bouncy or dead – and all of these conditions change during the course of a match, especially if it rains. This is why it features in the tactics on page 81.

Balls which don't bounce are called <u>full tosses</u> and the batsman's eyes usually light up with pleasure if he sees a full toss coming his way because it is probably easy to hit. Balls which don't bounce and veer towards the batsman above chest height are called <u>beamers</u>: these are not allowed, because they are dangerous, but they do sometimes happen by 'accident'. A beamer may be a no ball and count as one extra, but this is no consolation to the batsman who ends up in Casualty.

How does the captain decide which type of bowler to choose?

The captain usually likes to have different types of bowler in his team. This helps to break the concentration of the batsmen. It also gives him a wider range of tactics that he can use.

---

5 CRICKETERS WITH NAMES FROM SHAKESPEARE

- Duncan (Australia and *Macbeth*)

- Edgar (New Zealand and *King Lear*)

- Bottom (Derbyshire and *A Midsummer Night's Dream*)

- Gower (England, *Henry V* and *Pericles*)

- Julius Caesar (Surrey and *Julius Caesar*)

One reason for having a variety of bowlers is that different types of pitches help different types of bowlers. At the beginning of a match, the pitch may be flat, hard and bouncy, which is good news for fast bowlers. At the end it may have become rough and lumpy, which almost always helps the slow spin bowlers. The captain may even want to bring on a different type of bowler because of a change in the weather. Would you believe that some bowlers perform better when it is cloudy? (See 'Why do bowlers rub the ball on their trousers?' page 62.)

The condition of the ball also influences the captain when he is deciding who should bowl. The leather cricket ball has a prominent stitched <u>seam</u> around its middle, and at the start of a match the ball is <u>new</u> and shiny. Fast bowlers prefer the ball when it is hard and shiny, and spinners like it later on when it has been roughed up a bit, because it is easier to grip.

Who are the bowlers with long run ups?

The bowlers with long run ups are usually (but not always) the fastest, and they tend to start the bowling in an innings. Strange as it may seem, bowlers don't necessarily need a long run up to be fast: some famous bowlers like Malcolm Marshall have often bowled off a short run and still bowled at eighty or ninety miles per hour. The length of run up is all to do with rhythm, intimidation and ego.

The West Indies usually have more fast bowlers than anybody else. There always seem to be four world class fast bowlers in any West Indies team. It's a bit tough for the poor batsmen who, over the last twenty years, have had no respite.

Fast bowlers rely first and foremost on speed to beat a batsman. Speed means the batsman has less time to get his bat behind the ball, and it also increases the element of fear. This is heightened by the fact that, increasingly, fast bowlers make use of the bouncer which is pitched short and rears up at the batsman's head. The bouncer is most often bowled simply to frighten the batsman (who will usually duck underneath it). Sometimes a bouncer is bowled deliberately to induce a batsman to play a hook shot, with the hope that the ball will hit the edge of the bat and fly to a carefully placed fielder.

The wicket-keeper always stands well back from the stumps to a fast bowler – sometimes twenty yards or more.

What is a medium pacer?

Medium pacers, being slower than the fast bowlers, tend to be slightly more defensive. They will tend to have fewer slip fielders and more fielders in the covers (see 'Fielders' page 67). The medium, or medium fast, bowler relies a lot on his ability to make the ball *not* go in a straight line (deviate) – either by making it curve in the air (swing) or bounce funnily off the pitch. Sometimes he can make it do both prodigiously – how he does this is described in the next sections.

The wicket-keeper will sometimes stand close to the stumps for the medium pacer, so that he can intimidate the batsman with the possibility of a stumping (see page 35 for a reminder). Well, the batsman may be intimidated but the medium pacer is almost certainly insulted when this happens. Most medium pacers like to think of themselves as fast, and don't like the wicket-keeper to make a public gesture to contradict this.

Medium pacers have one major advantage over fast bowlers – they don't get tired as quickly. Sometimes the medium pacer is known as a stock bowler, someone who can bowl twenty or thirty overs a day with the aim of keeping one end going without conceding too many runs.

By the way, everything is relative: if you were to face a so-called medium pacer (Derek Pringle is a famous example) you would probably find him frighteningly fast.

Why do bowlers rub the ball on their trousers?

Some bowlers, particularly medium pacers, are able to make the ball swerve or swing in the air – away from the batsman or towards the batsman (out-swing and in-swing respectively).

So how does the ball swing? Physicists say that swing occurs when the half of the ball on one side of the seam is smooth and shiny while the other half is rough and dull. As the ball floats through the air, the rough side creates more air turbulence, slowing that side down, thus causing the ball to swing (a bit like using one oar to turn a boat).

Got it? If you haven't, never mind – just accept that the ball swings. (That's what most cricketers do!)

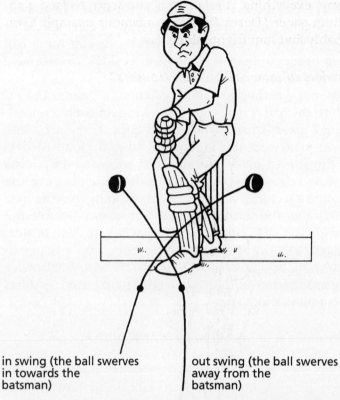

in swing (the ball swerves
in towards the
batsman)

out swing (the ball swerves
away from the
batsman)

This is why bowlers – particularly bowlers with long run ups – vigorously shine one half of the ball on their trousers, leaving a permanent red smear stain. Why, you might be asking, do they

---

5 FILM STARS WHO LOVED CRICKET

- David Niven
- Boris Karloff
- Basil Rathbone
- Errol Flynn
- Peggy Ashcroft

use that part of the trousers rather than, say, the shirt. The answer is entirely innocent (in my own case anyway – I can't speak for anyone else): it's the easiest place in which one can rub a ball vigorously in order to make it shiny. And besides, trousers are made from tougher material than shirts.

Cloudy, humid weather and swing often go together. In certain conditions the ball actually starts to swing almost uncontrollably, carving a great banana swathe as it goes. There are some commentators who reckon that it only takes a cloud to pass in front of the sun to make the ball start to swing. Physicists could have a field day explaining that one. Because of swing, the weather is often a factor considered when winning the toss (see 'Tactics'), although the strange thing is how unpredictable the degree of swing is. I've known the ball to swing more on beautiful sunny days than on heavily overcast days, and I begin to suspect that swing bowling has as much to do with the bowler being 'in a good rhythm' and the actual ball being used, as it has to do with cumulus and cirrus.

How do they make it bounce funnily off the pitch?

Some medium pace bowlers can make the ball deviate off the pitch, making them seam bowlers. In fact, most bowlers are capable of being seamers, simply because if the ball happens to land on the seam it will not bounce straight – the same as when a rugby ball bounces on its end, only not so pronounced.

Some bowlers are able to achieve considerable deviation of the ball towards and away from the batsmen (off and leg cutters), sometimes without knowing which it will be. Others help to produce this deviation by putting spin on the ball. There are a few bowlers around in the world who can bowl a fast leg break. However, most spin bowlers are slow bowlers (see next section).

There was much controversy in 1989 when Reader's, the ball makers, introduced a ball with a very large seam. This was used in county cricket, with the result that a lot of previously very ordinary bowlers suddenly started taking lots and lots of wickets. The following season the seam was reduced in thickness and the batsmen had a field day (and the bowlers a long-time-in-the-field day). The trouble with tampering with anything in cricket is that you're bound to upset the delicate balance of something or other...

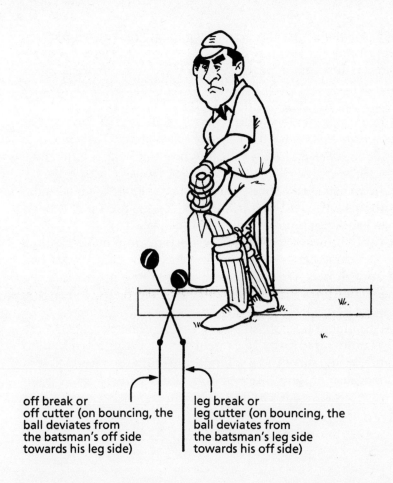

off break or
off cutter (on bouncing, the
ball deviates from
the batsman's off side
towards his leg side)

leg break or
leg cutter (on bouncing, the
ball deviates from
the batsman's leg side
towards his off side)

Aren't slow bowlers easy to hit?

The psychological game between the slow bowler and the batsman is one of the most fascinating parts of cricket. All the time the batsman is thinking, 'I should be able to hit one of these balls for six', while also fearing that if he tries, the ball may spin more than expected or be quicker and get him stumped, caught or whatever. The good slow bowler should therefore have the nerve to float the occasional ball high in the air, tempting the batsman to have a swipe.

Most serious slow bowlers are spinners: they impart a lot of spin to the ball as they release it, and the ball subsequently deviates off the pitch (see the illustration above). If you watch a

65

spinner on television, you may immediately be able to pick up this deviation. For some reason, the commentators have more trouble: a ball which appears to the viewer to have deviated by six inches from a straight line may evoke the comment 'Yes...I think that ball might have turned a little, Richie'. But whenever possible, commentators seem to want to deny that the ball has turned – especially if it's the first day of a match, when (because it is rolled so flat and hard) the pitch is not supposed to take spin.

Spinners come in two basic varieties: off spinners (whose main aim is to make the ball spin from off to leg for the right-handed batsman) and leg spinners (who do the opposite).

Most spin bowlers are off spinners – but some make it spin a lot more than others. An off spinner has a special type of ball called an arm ball which, rather than spinning in towards the batsman, continues in a straight line, or even drifts slightly the other way.

Most commentators go all gooey and sentimental when a leg spinner comes on to bowl, because it's like spotting a black rhino (rare and getting rarer). Leg spinners are certainly interesting to watch, because of their loopy action, and because a lot of good

---

5 CRICKETING LORDS

- Lord Beauclerk (1773-1850) – vicar of St Albans, an eccentric 'amateur' who claimed he could earn £600 a year from cricket

- Lord Harris (1851-1932) – MCC committee member who ruined the careers of several players because of his strictness on the no ball laws

- Lord Hawke (1860-1938) – prayed to God that no professional would ever captain England

- Lord Tennyson (1889-1951) – descendant of the poet. His valet was also his wicket-keeper

- 'Lord' Ted – nickname for Ted Dexter in the 1960s

batsmen don't know how to play them properly, and end up looking very silly. Richie Benaud, now a commentator, was one of the greatest leg spinners of all time.

Leg spinners (or leg break bowlers, or leggies) are very rare, partly because they have more difficulty controlling the ball and they are often expensive – they give away a lot of runs. A top class leg spinner is able to bowl other 'trick balls' including the top spinner, the flipper, and our friend the googly.

What is a googly?

By now you will be itching to know the answer to this question. In fact, since a picture paints a thousand words, before going any further you should look at the 'spot the difference' illustration on page 68 and all should become instantly clear.

Googlies are actually very rare. These days few cricket teams (be they professionals or village amateurs) have a leg spinner in the team, and even if they do he may well not be able to bowl an effective googly. This does not, however, prevent the word googly from frequently rearing its head in cricket conversation.

The word googly originated in Australia, but I can tell you no more than that: according to my dictionary its origin is 'obscure'. It was originally known as a bosie because it was invented in the early 1900s by BJT Bosanquet (who happened, incidentally, to be a relative of the late Reginald Bosanquet, the famous ITN newsreader).

While on the subject of obscure cricketing words, a left arm spinner sometimes bowls a chinaman, so named because the first bowler to bowl such a delivery was of Chinese extraction. Take diagram A on page 68 and look at it in a mirror. *That* is exactly what a chinaman looks like.

Fielders

How do they all know where to stand?

Before the bowler starts to bowl, the captain and bowler set the field (that is, they tell the fielders where to stand). This is one of the most important tactics of cricket (see page 82). The fielders are told to stand in the places where the captain thinks

SPOT THE DIFFERENCE

A

B

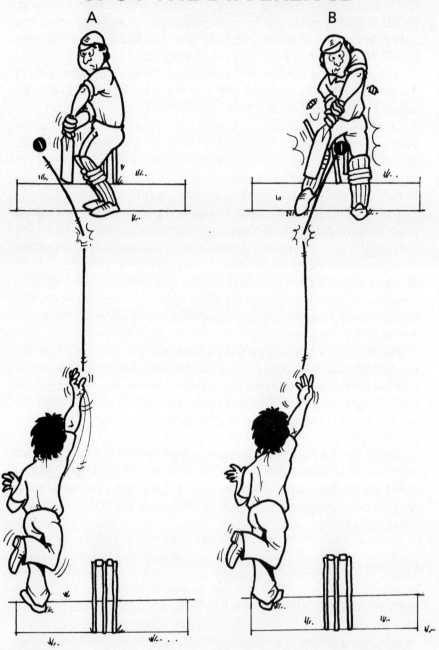

On the left, player A expects – and gets – a leg break (see page 64).
On the right, player B expects a leg break and gets…a GOOGLY!
The bowler subtly changes his hand action and the ball spins the
other way.

that the batsman is most likely to hit the ball: positions near to the batsman are called <u>attacking</u> (because the fielders are there in the hope of getting a catch); positions a long way from the batsman are called <u>defensive</u> (because the fielders are there to keep the number of runs down to a minimum).

Although all of the fielding positions have names, there are no marks on the field to say exactly where the fielding position is. So when the captain tells the fielder to stand at <u>extra cover</u>, say, the fielder wanders over in the general direction of where he thinks extra cover is, only to discover that the captain thinks it is somewhere twenty yards to the left. After a while, the fielder's position tends to drift from the original one anyway because he forgets where it was, but usually nobody notices this.

Fielders are normally asked to stand in positions suited to their own skills. Fielders with sharp reactions stand very close to the batsman. Fielders who are good at throwing the ball from a long way go somewhere near the boundary. Fielders who aren't very good at anything are put in as innocuous a position as possible, usually <u>mid on</u>, <u>mid off</u> or <u>square leg</u>. The overweight one usually stands at slip. (In village cricket, fielding at slip is something of a token gesture: nobody expects you to catch the ball.)

The most common positions where fielders stand are marked on the illustration on pages 70-71. Arrows have been added to indicate the vagueness of some of these positions.

What are 'silly mid off' and 'short leg'?

Some of the most amusing terminology in cricket comes from the fielding positions people stand in. Names like <u>silly mid off</u> and <u>short leg</u> are hard to take seriously (until you have to stand there, at which point you take them very seriously indeed if you value your life).

As you might expect, given cricket's eccentricities, there has been no great logic behind devising the names of fielding positions. Some are obvious enough: <u>square leg</u> is so-called because it is square to the wicket and it is on the leg side. But the fielder opposite square leg isn't called square off, he's called <u>point</u>. Cover is so called because he is there to 'cover' the ball if it is missed by the man standing at point. And extra cover is there to cover the man who is covering the man at point. As for <u>silly point</u> – this is so called because the fielder has to be pretty silly to stand there in the first place.

FIELDING

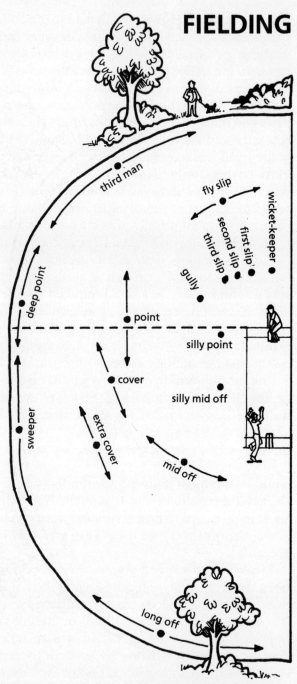

Note: *Fielding positions just above the dotted line in the diagram are called 'backward' and are 'behind square'; and those just below the dotted line are called 'forward' and are 'in front of square'. This is why you sometimes hear positions described as backward square*

POSITIONS

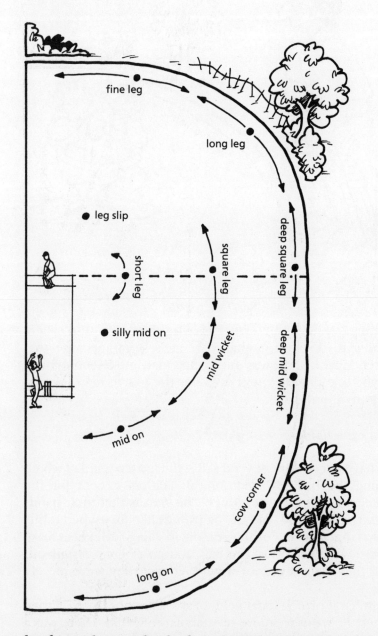

leg, forward square leg, backward point and so on.

You are only allowed to have two fielders behind square on the leg side. If three fielders stand there (for example at long leg, fine leg and leg slip), the umpire calls a no ball.

Fielding at silly point

One thing I've never understood is why 'third man' is so called. It's nothing to do with Graham Greene's story, because that came later. Maybe there was once a first man and a second man. And maybe one day they will discover the fourth man (or was that Anthony Blunt?)

Why don't the fielders wear gloves?

Fielders have to combine several skills, the most painful of which is stopping the ball. By tradition, all fielders except for the wicket-keeper do not wear gloves. This means that their hands can get extremely cold, and the ball stings like fury when it hits the hand at high speed. For this reason, in village cricket at least, fielders are often scared of the ball, and go to great lengths to look as if they have dived for it when in fact they were merely avoiding it.

By contrast if professional fielders are scared of the ball, they never show it. Many are quite spectacular to watch. There was a time (not long ago) when the team's fast bowler would be a terrible fielder: he would field at mid off, and would only be expected to make a half-hearted lean towards the ball before

trotting off to retrieve it from the boundary. Nowadays, partly because of the influence of one day cricket, nearly all professional fielders are great athletes and will dive to stop anything. Even if the ball is coming fast and is likely to break a bone, the fielder rarely takes evasive action. And it is actually a surprise to see catches dropped.

To increase the chance of stopping the ball (rather than letting it go through his legs) all fielders are taught to stop the ball by kneeling down on one knee and spreading the body behind the ball. This is all very well if the outfield is flat and even, but on cricket fields which are used for rugby in winter, the ball is prone to veer up towards the teeth on its last bounce. This is another good reason why any sane fielder looks somewhat tentative when the ball comes to him.

Because the ball comes to the wicket-keeper extremely often, and at high speed, he at least is allowed to wear pads and gloves. (Even then, he is often a victim of badly bruised fingers.)

Who is the twelfth man?

The twelfth man is nothing to do with the third man. (I hope this isn't getting too confusing.) In professional cricket (the sort you see on television), each team will always have eleven players on the field, and a twelfth player, known as the twelfth man, who spends most of the time sitting in the pavilion. The twelfth man is a cross between a substitute and a waiter: he can come on when one of the main eleven is – or claims to be – injured. It is also his job to bring on the drinks, protective clothing, messages from the pavilion etc.

In most amateur cricket there is rarely a twelfth man. This is because the person who picks the team has enough difficulty persuading eleven people to turn up for an afternoon, let alone a twelfth to act as slave.

Unless the twelfth man particularly enjoys fielding, his lot is not a very happy one: even when he is on the field replacing somebody, he is not allowed to bowl. Nor is he ever allowed to bat. Even if he takes a catch, his name is *never* put in the scorebook – instead it always appears as 'Sub'.

Umpires

What does the umpire do?

There are always two umpires on the field – one in charge of each end of the pitch. One umpire stands at the bowler's end and the other stands at the same position as the square leg fielder. The job of the umpire at the bowler's end is the more onerous, because not only does he have to make split-second decisions on appeals for LBW, he also has to watch the bowler's feet (looking for no balls), count the number of balls in the over (he usually carries six pebbles in his pocket to help him) and signal to the scorers if there is a boundary or an extra.

At the end of the over, however, he walks out to the square leg position, while the umpire in charge of the other end moves from what was square leg to stand at the other bowler's end. (Of course you will have realized that when the fielders change ends, the bit of grass that *was* square leg now becomes mid off. Check the diagram on page 70-71 if you need to prove this to yourself.)

It is also the duty of both umpires to carry the fielders' sweaters. This can be very tough on the poor umpire: when it is cold, all the fielders wear their sweaters so the umpire shivers. When it warms up, the fielders all give their sweaters to the umpire, who then swelters.

The umpires also have to try to apply the Laws of cricket to any obscure incident that happens in a match. For example, in 1899 two teams of soldiers were playing a match in India dressed in full uniform. A batsman hit the ball high into the air, and the fielder lost sight of it. The next thing he knew it had landed on his head and impaled itself on the spike on his helmet. The umpires consulted and decided to give the batsman out caught because the fielder had not *deliberately* used his helmet to catch the ball.

More recently, in 1980, a batsman in a Yorkshire club hit the ball in the air, and just as the fielder was about to catch it the batsman called to his colleague: 'It's all right, that one's safe.' The fielder, of course, did drop it, then appealed – and the umpires decided that the batsman had deliberately put the fielder off: he was given out 'obstructing the field'.

As you can see, the umpires always have to be on their toes for the unexpected.

COMMON UMPIRE SIGNALS

no ball

bye

leg bye

wide

four runs

six runs

out

(old cricket joke)

Who are the umpires?

In most 'friendly' village cricket, the two umpires are members of the batting team and are therefore (despite their honourable intentions) grossly biased. Umpiring for your team is not an enviable task, because it may involve making awkward decisions. Most umpires faced with a choice of giving out a member of their own team LBW or incurring the wrath of the opposition by saying 'not out' will opt for the latter. At least the opposition won't be seen for another year.

In professional and serious club cricket the umpires are independent and usually paid. They sometimes have the temperament of the officious traffic warden: they know the rules, and seem to take great delight in imposing them to the letter.

Usually professional umpires are only accused of bias in international cricket. By tradition, the umpires come from the host nation. This has often led to major rows, and every year without fail one country or another puts its defeat down to the incompetence or cheating of the host umpires. (In fact, you may recall that in 1987 there was a huge diplomatic incident when England captain Mike Gatting and Pakistani umpire Shakoor Rana accused each other of all sorts of things, including a few words that do not appear in this book's glossary. It didn't do much for either of their careers.) This is why there are now moves towards an international panel of independent umpires.

Professional umpires are almost always retired players (at any level of the game). Quite simply, it is of enormous help to understand how the players think, and more importantly, how they try to cheat. There's no better qualification than to be a poacher-turned-game-keeper. Umpires are therefore usually older than the players, which occasions some of the abuse they get. The joke goes 'I used to be a player, but then my eyesight and hearing went, so I became an umpire'.

Finally, two of the most famous and popular umpires. The first is Harold (Dicky) Bird, who is a great crowd-pleaser, except when it comes to taking out his light meter (which happens depressingly often). The second is David Shepherd, a large, jovial figure who follows an old Gloucestershire superstition concerning the number 111 (Nelson) and multiples thereof. The superstition is that if the score is on 111, 222 etc, a wicket will fall unless all the team, except the batsman at the crease, have their feet off the ground. Umpire Shepherd therefore hops in the air until the score changes. Who said they don't make characters like they used to?

6

What About Tactics?

What keeps the spectators so interested?

You may well have wondered in the past how anybody could seriously spend a day watching cricket without getting bored. (In fact, an American friend of mine took great delight in taking a camera to a match at Lord's – not to photograph the action, but to pick out people in the crowd who had fallen asleep or were buried in their newspapers.)

Surprising as it may seem, however, to many cricket fans the game is totally absorbing. One thing that makes it particularly interesting to its devotees is the use of tactics. Not only does a cricket captain probably have a wider range of tactics at his dis-

posal than in any other sport, he can also change the tactics after every ball. Thus, one over of just six balls can have been a series of mini-tactical ploys, all with the ultimate (but not necessarily immediate) intention of getting the batsman out. A bowler may play with a batsman in just the same way as a cat plays with a bird before it kills it…

Because each ball takes at least thirty seconds to happen, the spectator has a chance to watch the tactic being executed, to see its result and to comment on it to his colleague (if he has one). Given that the spectator is also busy filling in a scorecard, listening on his Walkman to what the radio commentators are saying about the tactic being used, and studying the players through his binoculars, one could even say that far from being too slow, cricket actually happens too quickly for the devoted cricket watcher to be able to take everything in. At the moment you might not see it that way. Who knows, maybe you will one day.

The tactics of the captains, the batsmen and the bowlers are a source of great fascination to the devoted cricket fan. Over a long period it is possible to get a good feel for each player's own particular style and tactics: is he adventurous? Does he panic? Does he act as though he really doesn't care?

The trouble is that, since few of us are able to mind-read, it can be difficult to understand what the tactics are at any particular time. Sometimes you will hear the commentators all agreeing that 'Really, he should be using a second slip fielder', yet the captain continues to adopt a completely different approach. Is he really so stupid? If so, there are very few captains who are worthy of the job, since almost all of them receive a constant stream of unheeded advice from beyond the boundary.

The truth is that:

- there is more than one way to skin a cat – and sometimes the least expected is the most successful;

- spectators aren't happy unless they are able to show themselves to be superior in thought to the men on the field;

and

- being captain isn't nearly as easy as it looks.

Anyway, let's look at some of the tactics employed by the various players which will reveal some of the finer points of cricket.

What does the captain do?

The overall strategy by which the team aims to win a match is determined by the captain (or if it isn't, he certainly gets the blame if it goes wrong). This all starts with perhaps the most significant part of all…

The toss (and the pitch)

At the beginning of the match the two captains toss a coin and the winner decides whether his team will bat or bowl first. Although winning the toss is luck, what the toss-winner decides to do next is a matter of skill, judgement and bluff. Whether his decision proves to be *right* is a combination of skill and an enormous amount of luck.

Before the toss, you will see captain and players carefully examining the pitch to decide what it is going to do, how it will

pitch inspection

change through the course of the game, etc. The whole subject of pitch inspection is the basis of an enormous pseudo-science. It's a bit like wine tasting. Players will stand around the pitch and will say things like 'it's a bit green' and 'this one will help the spinners' while the others all nod very sagely. But the fact is (and I won't make many friends with this statement) that I have met very few people who have been able to predict with any accuracy what a pitch was going to do.

What you can be pretty sure of, though, is that the pitch will become slower, more uneven and more cracked as the match progresses. More often than not this means it will become harder to bat on, which is why captains very often choose to bat first.

However, they don't always do so. If the weather is very overcast, the captain very often thinks: 'The ball is going to swing today, making it difficult to bat. I will put the other team in to bat first.' This theory sometimes works, but sometimes it fails completely: in 1989, at Leeds, England won the toss and asked Australia to bat first on a cloudy day. England lost. In 1991, also at Leeds, the West Indies won the toss and asked England to bat first on a cloudy day. The West Indies lost.

Tactics of the fielding captain

Being captain when your team is fielding is an arduous task. First of all there is the job of motivating your team. Fielders often use the time they spend wandering around the boundary to philosophise about life – which means that their minds may drift from the cricket in progress. The captain does what he can to motivate remote fielders, usually by clapping his hands and shouting something stirring like, 'Come on, lads, on your toes'. He also has to plan his field so that the fielder on one boundary doesn't have to run to the other side of the field at the end of the over – which is extremely de-motivating.

tactics are sometimes discussed in advance

The captain may also have to keep motivating his bowlers, particularly fast bowlers (who have a reputation for being sensitive souls). Motivating the bowler may involve running up to him after every ball, patting him on the back and saying – 'Well done, but pitch it up next time and he won't hit you for four'. In contrast, though, ex-England captain Mike Brearley used to motivate Ian Botham by threatening to take him off. Botham would immediately take a wicket.

The tactics of the fielding captain will also include:

- setting an attacking field (usually lots of fielders very close to the batsman to intimidate him, or entice him into playing an attacking shot – and with any luck missing);

- setting a defensive field (fielders a long way from the bat, frustrating the batsman because it becomes hard to score runs, so the batsman eventually does something silly – and misses);

- putting on a fast bowler (because the batsman is known to be weak against fast bowling);

- putting on a slow bowler (who can induce a false shot through guile and variety);

- putting on an extremely slow – not to say rubbish – bowler (who can induce a false shot because all batsmen wrongly assume they can hit a rubbish bowler for six every time);

- bringing on the same bowler from the opposite end, unsettling the batsman who has got used to seeing this bowler with a particular tree behind his left shoulder. (Note that a bowler cannot bowl consecutive overs, so a different bowler – a change bowler – may be brought on for just one over to enable his colleague to change ends. This is another tactic.)

Tactics of the batting captain

The tactics of the batting captain are more limited. To some extent once his chaps are out there there is precious little he can do about it. The main tactics he employs concern deciding when to declare (see page 44), which order to send his batsmen in to bat, and what instructions to give them before they go.

The instruction he gives to a batsman is likely to be one of: 'just stay in there'; 'keep it steady, nothing too rash'; 'start pushing the score along'; or 'take a look at a couple of balls, then hit out'. Occasionally, instructions may change during a batsman's innings, in which case the twelfth man is sent out under the pretext of perhaps taking a drink to the batsman, but also carrying a message with the change of plan. Since it is hard for most batsmen to adjust their natural game (which may be attacking or defensive), following the captain's instructions can often be counter-productive: the batsman gets out, which is what nobody wanted.

Things always get a little tense when lunch, tea or bed is approaching. The batsmen don't want to get out at this stage, and certainly no batsman wants to start his innings with only five minutes to go before a break. It takes a batsman quite a while to 'get his eye in' when he starts his innings, or at the start of the day.

For this reason, if a wicket falls within twenty minutes of the end of the day, the captain will often send in what is known as the night watchman. This is a batsman who is not particularly good but is good enough to be able to survive, without necessarily scoring any runs, for twenty minutes. The night watchman has less to lose if he gets out, and protects a good batsman from coming in when the pressure is on late in the evening. It has been known for a night watchman to go on and score fifty; and it has

night watchman

been known for a second night watchman to be sent in because the first failed to do his job properly.

What goes through the mind of the bowler?

As well as following the tactics of the captain, the individual bowler will (if he has any nous, and one does sometimes wonder) also be employing tactics. Two of the greatest bowling tacticians of recent times have been Sir Richard Hadlee and Malcolm Marshall. Both fast bowlers, they became renowned for regularly out-smarting batsmen, not by trying to bowl every ball at the batsman at one hundred miles per hour, but by always keeping batsmen wondering what the next ball would do.

The bowler tries to <u>beat</u> the batsman or induce him to play a

false stroke. He can do this either by sheer pace and hostility, by deception, or by frustration. Most bowlers have to settle for the last two.

Deception is achieved by using one of the three main arts in bowling: the ability to bowl at varying speeds; the ability to vary the flight of the ball (i.e. make it lob high in the air or shoot through quite flat); and the ability to make the ball deviate from going in a straight line (in the air or when it bounces off the pitch). A few bowlers can do none of these very much, and have to concentrate on always bowling straight at the stumps, to keep the batsman at bay. Fred Trueman calls this 'bowlin' line and len'th'. Apparently this is what all bowlers did in his day – as well as getting up at five o'clock every morning, walking twenty miles to t'ground and bowling uphill all day into a Force Eight gale. But they were 'appy.

The bowler has a number of skills at his disposal (see page 58), but in essence – if he is very skilful – he will be able to decide before each ball which of the following he wants to do:

- make the ball move in towards the batsman;

- make the ball move away from the batsman;

- scare the batsman with a bouncer;

- make the ball bounce very close to the batsman's toes (these balls are hard to hit, and are called yorkers – often a bouncer is followed immediately by a yorker);

---

5 CRICKETING FISH

- G H Salmon (Leicestershire)

- E F Herring (Oxford University)

- C A Roach (West Indies)

- A Pike (Nottinghamshire)

- C R D Rudd (Eton and Oxford)

- aim to hit the stumps (bowl <u>straight</u>);

- aim well wide of the stumps, encouraging the batsman to chase the ball with an attacking shot;

- bowl from a slightly different angle, very close to or well wide of the umpire;

- bowl a <u>slower ball</u> (the batsman, expecting a normal speed ball, will with any luck swing at the ball too early and miss);

- instead of running up past the left* hand side of the umpire (known as <u>over the wicket</u>), change direction by running up past the right* hand side of the umpire (<u>round the wicket</u>). Such a change often means the batsman also has to have the <u>sightscreen</u> behind the bowler moved across.

As you can see, there are lots of things that can happen, and in combination they can all help to unsettle a batsman so much that he becomes uncertain about which shot to play and is finally out.

It is not always the good ball that takes a wicket: sometimes it is what seems to be a very bad ball. This is why it is important to judge an incident in cricket by its *context*, since one bad shot could well be the result of a sustained period of very good bowling. (On the other hand, it might just be a bad shot.) This is

---

5 TOPICS OCCASIONALLY DISCUSSED BY THE RADIO 3 CRICKET COMMENTARY TEAM

- The colour of the local buses

- The weather

- Mrs Ramsbottom's delicious cream cake

- The Primary Club

- The cricket match that is taking place

---

* Other way round if the bowler bowls with his left arm.

why the purists tend to be very dismissive of the so-called high-lights of the day, which are usually shown at some ungodly hour on BBC2. The highlights consist of batsmen hitting boundaries (viewed by cameras from about six different angles) and bowlers taking wickets (from even more angles). Of course cricket, like life, isn't like that.

It may be that the best tactical bowler merely prevents the batsmen from scoring, while a worse bowler at the other end takes less deserved wickets. From the viewpoint of the captain, this is fine. From the viewpoint of the good bowler, this is very irritating, since the statistics from the match will say nothing about how well he bowled. Still, both Hadlee and Marshall have phenomenally good statistical records, so it must all come out in the wash eventually.

What are the batsman's tactics?

The tactics of the batsman are a little less sophisticated simply because he is having to react to the tactics of the bowler. The batsman is not in a position before every ball to say, 'I'm going to hit this for six'. This is because the bowler may, for example, bowl a yorker which it is not possible to hit for six. The batsman, as he stands out there nervously pacing up and down, twirling his bat, prodding an imaginary divot on the pitch, or whatever else he does to spin out time between deliveries, is developing a general strategy that will evolve through his innings according to the state of the game at any one time.

This might go as follows:

[Early in his innings] I must not get out or I won't be able to look my mates in the eye. I will defend any straight balls, and leave everything that isn't going to hit my stumps.

[Ten minutes later] OK, I'm settled now: if there is a bad ball, I will try to hit it through that gap at mid off.

[Thirty minutes later] Ah, they've brought on a slow bowler – a chance for me to play a very attacking shot to show who is boss.

[He's been in for two hours] Right, I've scored my fifty. I'm feeling confident so I will start getting more aggressive now.

[Two hours later] I'm knackered. Still, every time I swing my bat I seem to score runs, so I'll keep going.

Of course, any attempt to put a time against each tactic is an over-simplification. Some batsmen go on the attack right at the beginning. Others seem to be slow and cautious even when they are 150 not out.

The batsman's tactics may also change at a moment's notice, in particular:

- when he is close to 50 or 100;
- when lunch, tea or bed-time (close of play) is fast approaching;
- when the man at the other end is out.

In each of these cases, the normal practice is to revert to not taking risks and therefore scoring more slowly. Thankfully, there are a few cricketers around who are prepared to take risks at any time. Most of them are Indian or West Indian. They are exciting to watch but if it all goes wrong, their fans can be pretty unforgiving.

Finally, before you blame a batsman for indiscretion or incompetence, remember that while a bowler has at least thirty seconds to change his mind about what to do with the next ball, a batsman often has only a fraction of a second.

So is there some kind of master plan?

All of the above tactics help towards the one overall objective of cricket: winning, or at least, not losing. (In village cricket, the captain may have another conflicting objective, which is to make sure everyone in his team gets to do something: this may mean giving old Bert a chance to bowl, which may actually contribute to the defeat of his team.)

If his team bats first, the captain who wants to win has to try to ensure that he gives his bowlers enough time to bowl out the opponents later on (see 'Who's winning?' page 41).

It is usually easier to get opponents out if they are trying to score runs and so taking risks. Therefore, unless the captain believes his bowlers can get batsmen out even when they are playing defensively, he may have to tempt the batsmen with the possibility of victory by making it apparently easy or safe for the batsmen to try to score runs. This is why a bowler who looks very slow and easy to hit is sometimes brought on to bowl:

- the slow bowler looks rubbish but is good, thus fooling the batsman into getting out;

● the slow bowler *is* rubbish, enabling the batsmen to score enough runs to give them just a sniff of victory (and hence give the bowlers the chance of getting them out later on).

(There are other much more subtle reasons for bringing on slow bowlers, see page 65).

When, in village cricket, old Bert is brought on to bowl merely so that he can be made to feel that he has contributed to the game, this can sometimes pay off as a tactic. This is because the batsman gets over-confident, pictures the ball sailing into the duck pond, takes an almighty swipe with his head in the air – and misses the ball. If this happens everyone except the batsman's relatives is allowed to laugh.

The other most common tactic to bring about a win is to declare. The captain finishes his team's innings before all of his batsmen are out to give himself time to bowl out the opposition. There may be an element of risk in declaring, if not enough runs have been scored. Once the captain has declared, he can't later change his mind and ask if his batsmen can go back in.

7

Do Cricket Matches Last For Ever?

In the old days it was possible for a cricket match to last for ever. Nowadays, to the reluctant spectator, it only *seems* that way. The so-called Timeless Test in Durban in 1939 dragged on for ten days before England had to abandon it (as a draw) so that they could catch the boat home, but these days a time limit (or alternatively an overs limit) is put on every game of cricket so that everybody knows the latest that it will finish.

The different types of cricket all last a different length of time. The type which lasts the longest is two innings cricket (that is, both teams are allowed to bat twice). This is usually only played by professionals. Two innings cricket is almost always classified as <u>first class</u> cricket. And to the cricket buff, first class cricket means *proper* cricket.

Most other matches, especially those played by your average village club, are one innings matches, and last for one day or less. Limited overs matches are a special type of one innings match designed to ensure that one or other side wins. They are also known as 'one day cricket', although the English weather means that one day cricket sometimes takes two days. Another cricket eccentricity.

If you want more details on all of these types of cricket, then read on…

What is Test cricket?

Test cricket is the slowest version of cricket (in terms of number of incidents per minute). It can also last up to five days. To most real cricket enthusiasts, however, Test cricket is the most important version of the game, because it is played by the best cricketers and those cricketers take it all very seriously – which means that the tactics are very important.

Test cricket effectively means international cricket, although only those countries that are deemed to have reached the required level of skill are given Test status. There are now eight Test-playing countries:

⚉ Australia, England, India, New Zealand, Pakistan, South Africa, Sri Lanka and the West Indies.

At least one Test country tours England every summer and at least one Test match is played at Lord's. Lord's is located in St John's Wood, London. It is known as the home of cricket, and is one of the most pleasant sporting stadia in the world.

The only other grounds where Tests are played in England are: The Oval (South London), Headingley (Leeds), Old Trafford (Manchester), Trent Bridge (Nottingham) and Edgbaston (Birmingham).

Most Test matches are played in a sequence of three or five matches known as a series (or sometimes a rubber). Any series between England and Australia, however, is known as The Ashes. This dates back to 1882, when Australia thrashed England in a Test match, and the *Sporting Times* published a mock obituary

---

5 PERFECT HOLIDAYS: THE SEASIDE *AND* A GAME OF COUNTY CRICKET

⚉ Southend-on-Sea

⚉ Weston-super-Mare

⚉ Blackpool

⚉ Hove

⚉ Scarborough

of English cricket, saying that the ashes would be taken to Australia. The next winter, England went out to reclaim these metaphorical ashes. England won this series of matches two–one, and some enterprising women from Melbourne presented the England captain with a four-inch-high trophy containing some real ashes. This tiny trophy – which now lives in a glass case at Lord's – has become the symbol of one of the most hard fought and long standing of all international competitions.

Because Test cricket is regarded by players and public alike as the highest form of cricket, it is played much more seriously: you will observe that compared to most other cricket, the batsmen are more careful, the umpires study the light with greater scrutiny, and the rate at which runs are scored can sometimes be painfully slow. The crowds are usually big and the corporate hospitality suites are packed (especially on weekdays).

If you watch a full day of a Test match and see 300 runs being scored, it is generally felt that you got your money's worth. At up to twenty pounds for a good seat, that puts runs at about seven pence each – although there are those who would pay twenty pounds just to see one exquisite shot by David Gower.

Big crowds go to watch the first three days of a Test match (in England these are always Thursday, Friday and Saturday). However, attendance on the fourth and fifth days usually ranges from the disappointing to the non-existent. The reason for this is partly that there is no guarantee that the match will last for all five days, and partly because the game is generally deemed to be more interesting in its early development than in its dénouement. In fact, the last day is sometimes the most exciting part of a Test match, and tickets are always much cheaper. If you ever want to sample Test cricket and think you would find a big crowd of cricket enthusiasts a bit intimidating, go to the fifth day of a Test.

Which counties play county cricket?

First class county cricket is now played by eighteen teams, Durham having joined in 1992, and does much to keep alive memories of what England was like before they re-drew the county boundaries. The eighteen are: Derbyshire, Durham, Essex, Glamorgan, Gloucestershire, Hampshire, Kent, Lancashire, Leicestershire, Middlesex, Northamptonshire (Northants), Nottinghamshire (Notts), Somerset, Surrey, Sussex, Warwickshire, Worcestershire, Yorkshire. All other counties are known as Minor Counties, and play mostly amateur (but very serious) cricket between themselves.

To encourage home grown talent to play county cricket, the counties are only allowed to have one overseas player playing in the team at any one time. Until 1992, Yorkshire did not allow any overseas players – or any non-Yorkshiremen for that matter – to play for it at all. This is one reason why Yorkshire often finished near to the bottom of the county championship. Note that the England Test team can include players from Glamorgan (and indeed from the rest of Wales, and also Scotland).

Counties make a lot of their money from one day cricket – each year they play the NatWest Trophy, the Benson & Hedges Cup and the Sunday League – but it is the County Championship which is the backbone of professional cricket in England. County matches last either three or four days, and there are two innings for each team. The matches often have exciting finishes because the teams get lots of points for winning and hardly any points for a draw. However, whereas First or Premier Division soccer regularly makes an appearance on telly, its equivalent in cricket – the County Championship – ticks along with hardly any television interest at all. One reason is that not many people go to watch county cricket these days, and if there is one thing that a producer hates, it is televising an event at which there are no spectators.

There are exceptions though: go to Worcester on a sunny day and the pretty ground, which sits in the shadow of the cathedral, is often almost packed. Other attractive grounds that do well include Canterbury, Chesterfield, Chelmsford and Arundel. But Middlesbrough on a cold Monday afternoon has rather less appeal.

Three and four day county cricket provides the backbone to English cricket. It also has an important social function, as anyone who has had the pleasure of attending one of the many annual cricket festivals – such as Cheltenham or Scarborough – will happily tell you. Unfortunately, because of the relatively small crowds that most championship games attract, county clubs now depend for their survival on sponsorship and on the income gained from one day cricket and Test cricket. But here are some things county clubs could do to boost their attendances:

- provide decent food on the ground, instead of the greasy burger bar that is usually to be found;

- provide spectators with somewhere civilized to shelter and socialize when it is raining;

- make an effort to attract the casual visitor or tourist who has never entered a cricket ground;

- for those games where only twenty spectators are expected, why not reduce the price of tickets and attract a few more?

Which is the type of cricket that almost looks interesting?

If, as somebody who doesn't like cricket, you have ever found yourself watching a match for more than ten minutes, the chances are that it was a limited overs (otherwise known as a 'one day') match – because, superficially, this form of cricket is more interesting. (In other words, it is easier to tell that things are happening.) In Australia and New Zealand, you can spot a game of limited overs cricket because instead of wearing white, the players usually wear coloured clothing, earning this version of the game the nickname pyjama cricket. You may have noticed that the last World Cup was played in pyjamas.

This sort of cricket usually finishes in one day (and, in Australia, often under floodlights). Unlike other forms of cricket, the end of the match is not determined by the clock, but by the number of overs that have been bowled. Each team is given a fixed maximum number of overs (usually between forty and sixty) to score as many runs as possible. Of course the team may be all out before its overs have finished, which means that its innings finishes early. And it is *impossible to draw* a limited overs game: the team with the most runs at the end wins. Even if rain stops play, they always have a way of working out (or guessing) which team would have won, and giving them the prize.

Limited overs cricket is a relatively new phenomenon: it only began in earnest in 1963, which in cricketing terms is extremely recently. Despite that, it has taken over from proper cricket far more than anyone could have conceived. The spectators like it because more runs and more exciting finishes can be guaranteed, they can make more noise, and there is always a winner or loser. More sixes are hit, and there are more run outs. It is easier to feel the tension, because it builds up as the overs tick by, and you can calculate at any stage exactly what rate is

less elegant strokeplay

required to win the match. You can even ask, 'Who's winning?' (Well, almost.)

But what limited overs cricket lacks is some of the more intriguing and subtle elements of other forms of cricket: you will never see attacking fielding positions such as silly mid off or even third slip; nor will you see a night watchman; and almost certainly you won't see a leg spin bowler, let alone his googly (unless the bowler's name is Mushtaq…). The statistics in this form of cricket are usually meaningless, because in the frantic chase to score runs (especially near the end of the innings), batsmen are less concerned about losing their wickets. And the radio commentary loses a lot of that special wit and sparkle when limited overs cricket is being played.

Every year, more and more international one day matches seem to be played. In Australia, they hold an annual competition called the World Series Cup. This requires a rather loose interpretation of the word 'World', since World Series cricket only involves three countries – Australia plus any other two that it can persuade to come along.

World Series cricket should not be confused with the World Cup, the limited overs competition which is run every four years between all the main cricketing countries. When it was first invented (in 1975), the World Cup was quite a charming, innocent competition. Unfortunately that innocence has now been lost. The hype these days tells us that the World Cup is now the most important cricket competition. Cynics would replace the word 'important' with the word 'commercial'.

What type of cricket do they play on the village green?

The cricket played by the locals on the village green (or at the sports club) will be one of two types: league cricket in which the club is part of a local league, or friendly cricket where the people turn out simply for the love of playing cricket. The two types of cricket may be played on the same pitches, but there is a big difference. Friendly cricket is just that: the perfect English scene, with tea and scones being served in the pavilion, old Bert being given a chance to bowl, wives reading the newspaper, laughter when old Bert drops a catch, and children playing on the swings.

League cricket, on the other hand, is desperately serious. Drop a catch in league cricket, and you will be lucky if anybody in your team talks to you for the next six weeks. The faces in the pavilion look tense and rather grim. You don't play league cricket to enjoy yourself: you do it to prove yourself on the field, to win, or to take out your grudge on the rivals from the next town. League cricket in certain regions (Lancashire and the West Midlands spring to mind) is played to a high standard and often the club will have enough funds to be able to afford a professional, who may be an international player from another country.

You can usually tell which type of cricket is being played just by looking at the players. If they all walk in when the bowler runs up to bowl, and if they all look lean and mean – dressed immaculately in white – then you are watching league cricket, and probably the club's first eleven at that. On the other hand if you see beer guts, an assortment of different coloured cricket sweaters, a couple of rather static elder statesmen, a bowler with a short run up, and a keen looking ten-year-old boy standing at mid off – then you are almost certainly looking at a friendly match. Either that, or it's the club's third eleven which struggled to get a team together this week.

Because amateur cricketers don't have time to play cricket for more than a day or half-day at weekends, league and friendly cricket is almost always a one innings match which will end at about seven o'clock and could well be a draw. (Some club matches are limited overs, but these are in the minority.)

fielding after tea

All matches focus around tea, which plays an important part in the tactics of the game. The team which bats first knows that it will have to field after tea. Only the most dedicated of club players is able to resist the great spread of sponge cakes, scones, cheese and pickle sandwiches and sausage rolls supplied by the devoted tea-makers. The result of this is that the team batting second will benefit from at least half an hour of less than energetic fielding from their opponents.

Club cricketers like, where possible, to mimic the behaviour of the professionals they see on television. The batsmen turn up their collars and prod the pitch in just the same way as their heroes. The bowlers frantically rub the ball on their trousers. But what they can't copy is the quality of the pitch. Much village cricket is played on surfaces that have little in common with a billiard table. It's a good job that there aren't many very fast bowlers in village cricket, or you would hear of a lot more broken limbs than are actually suffered.

8

What About All Those Numbers?

You will note from everything that has been said so far that although cricket is a team game, the individual players may also be in it for themselves. In most team sports, like hockey and football, the success of the individual is closely tied to whether his team wins or not, but in cricket a player's own performance is often much more important to him than his team's performance.

The most obvious reason for this is that it is easier to measure the performance of a bowler and a batsman in cricket than of a full-back in football: in football, only the goals scored are recorded for posterity. In cricket, the number of runs scored by each player, how long he took to score them, how he was out, which bowler got him out, what time the rain came...all of these things are recorded with accountant-like accuracy.

Why do they like all those numbers?

To some people cricket is statistics. They live and breathe nothing but facts and figures: how many runs did Bradman score? Who was the only bowler to take nineteen wickets in a Test? Who was the only first class cricketer to have seven initials before his surname?

These statistics form the backbone of the Test Match Special radio commentary – in between the slices of chocolate cake and the occasional description of what is happening on the field. There are some who object to statistics on the grounds that they are usually irrelevant. On the other hand, some people like the statistics partly *because* they are so irrelevant.

If you hear Bill Frindall (without doubt the greatest statistician of them all) listing all the left-handed batsmen who have kept wicket for England at Headingley since the war, you may ask: so what? The answer is: exactly – so what!

Who keeps the score?

Wherever there is a serious cricket match taking place in any corner of the world, the details will be recorded in a book known as the scorebook. If you go to a village game, you will usually see one of the players religiously bent over a small book writing something. He is the scorer – scoring being a duty of members of the team which is marginally preferred to umpiring because you can do it sitting down, and you can still talk to your pals. (Professional teams, however, have their own full-time professional scorer.)

What the scorer is doing is noting down what happened after every ball: who bowled it, what the batsman scored off it, and what happened to the total. If nothing happens, the scorer puts a dot in the book (this is sometimes called a dot ball). If you were to look at details of most matches you would see an awful lot

---

5 *OTHER* CRICKET-LOVING PRIME MINISTERS

- Bob Menzies (Australia)
- Bob Hawke (Australia)
- Michael Manley (Jamaica)
- Alec Douglas-Home (United Kingdom)
- Clement Attlee (United Kingdom)

EXTRACTS FROM A SCOREBOOK

Details of every ball in the match are recorded in the scorebook.
This is what you might see if you looked over the scorer's shoulder.

	BATSMAN		HOW OUT	BOWLER	TOTAL
1	CRUSSELL	······1······1··11·······1······1·· / ··2·······	LBW	SPARKES	8
2	MAYHEW	·2·1··4·1·2·22·2·41·23···42·64·1· / 24··12·211·1··4··1	CT. BROWN	BAKER	62
3	HANSON.J.	··2···7·1··4···7··1·	BOWLED	KRAMER	10
4	JARVIS		RUN OUT		

Crussell and Mayhew were the opening batsmen. Crussell's innings had lots of dots in it – these are the balls he didn't score off. Not an exciting innings to watch. Mayhew, on the other hand, scored off almost every ball he faced – an extremely exciting innings. (By the way, scorers don't always record every 'dot' for the batsmen – it's too much effort.)

	BOWLER	1	2	3	4	5	6	7	8	9	10	OVERS	MDNS	RUNS	WKTS
1	SPARKES	M	M	··2 1·	M	M	··2 ··	W	2· 41	X		8	5	12	1
				0-3	0-3	0-3	0-5	1-5	1-12						
2	CRISP	·1 21 ··	·· 41 ·1	1· 22 2·	4· 11 ··	2· 3· 1·	46 24 ··		X			6	0	45	0
		0-4	0-10	0-17	0-23	0-29	0-45								
3	TROTTER	12 ·· ··	·4 2· 1·	·· 21 11	·2 2· ·1	M	4· ·1 ··	W· ·· 61	X			7	1	32	1
		0-3	0-10	0-15	0-20	0-20	0-25	1-32							
4	BAKER	41 2·	2· 1·	·1 1·	1·	··	··	2·1							

Sparkes and Crisp opened the bowling. Sparkes bowled extremely well – you can tell because of all the 'M's (maiden overs) and 'W's (wicket maidens) that he got. Only 12 runs were scored off his eight overs. Crisp, on the other hand, conceded 45 runs off just six overs, which no doubt incurred the wrath of his captain.

of dots, sometimes joined up to form an 'M' (signifying **maiden over**) or 'W' (**wicket maiden** over).

The scorer has to make periodic checks to see that everything adds up. After about half an hour it rarely does, at which point he applies his skills in creative accounting to making up the deficit of one run or more by finding a place to add a run which nobody will notice.

How do you know when to clap?

Apart from the obvious occasions when there is a good shot or a good catch or a maiden over, clapping normally happens when something or other adds up to fifty or a hundred. Hundreds always merit bigger claps than fifties. (Higher multiples of fifty are rarer, but also merit claps.)

You are allowed to clap when any of the following reach a

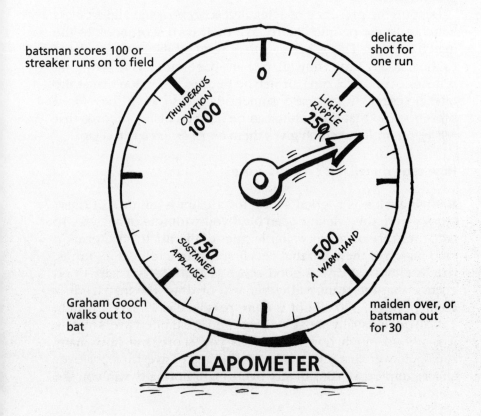

batsman scores 100 or
streaker runs on to field

delicate
shot for
one run

THUNDEROUS OVATION 1000

LIGHT RIPPLE 250

0

750 SUSTAINED APPLAUSE

500 A WARM HAND

Graham Gooch
walks out to
bat

maiden over, or
batsman out
for 30

CLAPOMETER

multiple of fifty (they are in descending order of importance and therefore size of clap):

- batsman's individual total (batsman will raise bat in acknowledgement);

- team's total;

- partnership between the two batsmen (i.e. number of runs scored since the last wicket fell).

Do *not* clap when the number of runs conceded by the bowler reaches fifty – it's not a statistic to be proud of.

The players on the pitch, and the public at large, are kept informed of the main elements of the score via a scoreboard. Reading most scoreboards is a skill in itself, and probably enough to put non-cricketers off trying to understand any more about the game. Every scoreboard will carry the bare essentials: the team's total, the number of wickets lost and, if appropriate, the number of overs. Anything else that appears on the scoreboard is background material.

Despite the presence of a detailed scoreboard at all first class matches, some people like to take their own scorebook to the match anyway. This is because they want all the detail available to them at any time (how many balls has Smith faced, how long is it since we saw a run), or maybe because they don't trust the official scorer. In any case, somebody has to keep the official scorebook so that the public can be notified of any records that are being broken, which gives them another excuse to clap.

How can you tell if it's a good score?

Knowing what is a 'good score' for a team is another of those areas where the cricketer can bluff you with lots of analysis. In fact, there are some very simple rules of thumb. In an afternoon club match, if the team that bats first scores a total of 200 runs, that is almost always a good score (i.e. there is a very good chance that the team will either win or draw the match). In a county match, 300 all out is quite reasonable. In a Test match, 350 all out is usually above average. And in a limited overs match, it is not so much how many runs you score, but how many runs per over that you score. An average of five runs per over (for example 250 runs in fifty overs) will normally win you the match.

THE SCOREBOARD

There are, of course, some exceptions. You would not expect to score nearly as many runs in any of the following conditions:

- if it is very cloudy and damp (this does all sorts of strange things to the ball and the pitch);

- if the pitch is very rough and unpredictable;

- if the opposition bowlers are very good.

In these conditions, a first innings of 200 in a Test match is quite respectable.

As for the rate at which things happen – well, in a Test match if a team scores at a rate of sixty runs per hour (or one run per minute) the crowd will usually leave with a very contented smile. Thirty runs per hour and they start to get fidgety. The other way of looking at this is that if the team has scored at more than three runs per over, the crowd will probably be satisfied, while with anything under two runs per over, tedium will set in and you will soon have a Mexican Wave on your hands.

Another rule of thumb is that a team is doing all right if it puts on about 35 runs per wicket. So if you see a score of 35 for 1, 70 for 2, 105 for 3 etc. up to 350 all out, then that is a reasonable score. Things never go this smoothly in practice though, so when you switch on the lunchtime news to hear that 'England have collapsed to 80 for 5 this morning' you should not be surprised. Nor should you be surprised to hear later on that England have 'recovered' to 220 for 7. The reporters tend to get a bit hysterical because it makes for better headlines, but batting collapses and recoveries are an essential part of cricket's drama.

Do I need to know any of the famous statistics?

You will notice when you listen to cricket commentators or other experts talking that they will often drop statistics into the conversation. For example, 'Did you know that this is the first time that Sproggett has scored a fifty on a Saturday at Old Trafford against Middlesex since his debut in 1981?'

Cricketers delight in recording unusual incidents that have happened in matches. Think of almost any freak event, and you can be sure that it has featured in a cricket match somewhere: teams have been all out for no runs, a single bowler has taken all ten wickets, batsmen have batted for five days without being out...and so on. The biggest score ever made was by a school-

AND AT THE END OF TODAY'S PLAY, ENGLAND FINISHED ON 171 FOR 6 ....

IS THAT GOOD OR BAD?

(Answer: probably bad. It depends!)

boy, in 1899. A E J Collins scored 628 not out over a period of several afternoons. That must have improved his average a bit.

And the records in first class cricket are almost as staggering: the highest score by a player in a Test match was 365 not out, by Gary Sobers in 1958. It took him ten hours and fourteen minutes. It was also Gary Sobers who once hit six sixes in a single over, when playing against Glamorgan. By a remarkable coincidence the television cameras were there, so poor old Malcolm Nash (the bowler on this occasion) has remained famous for all the wrong reasons.

I could go on with record statistics for many pages, but there is no need since they are all recorded in a book called the Wisden Cricketers' Almanack. This small, fat, yellow book, which is published every year, contains over 1,000 pages of statistics including details of every first class cricket match played anywhere in the world that year. It is known as the cricketer's bible.

Do you need to know such trivia? In terms of understanding the game, certainly not. Statistics do, however, help you to put what you are seeing into context – it is quite interesting to know that a batsman has never scored a century on this ground, say, because you then know that when he gets to 99 he will probably be even more nervous than normal. Knowing the statistics also gives more excuses to clap: there is always a knowledgeable ripple of applause around the ground when a batsman or bowler passes a previous record.

But unless you have a particular statistical bent, do not bother to learn any of these statistics. The more important ones will become familiar after a while, and you will begin to get a feel for what is or is not a significant achievement. In any case, television and radio commentators are so thorough with statistics that you are unlikely to miss anything if you are listening to either.

9

Am I Ready to go to a Match Now?

Now that you have read all the theory, the best thing to do is go along to see a real match. One option would be a Sunday League match played by your local county, which has the advantage that it all happens in one afternoon. Before you go to any match, however, there are certain things you ought to take with you, and certain points of etiquette to observe.

What should I take to a match?

First of all, take some food. Not only does food give you something to concentrate on when nothing else is happening, but also the sandwiches that you take will almost certainly be more wholesome than the fare you will be able to buy from the burger stand at the ground. (If you get yourself invited into the hospitality areas, of course, your own food will not be necessary – in fact nor will many other things be, since you will probably not be obliged to watch any of the cricket.)

Also take a drink, since the queues at the bar during the intervals between play can be appalling. A flask of hot tea is advisable during all but the most pleasant of English summers.

Other equipment if often a good idea, especially protection against the elements. What looks like a sunny day when you peer through the curtains in the morning can prove to be very cold when you are sitting in one place for much of the day. A sweater,

be prepared!

an umbrella and a waterproof jacket all prevent a day at the cricket from becoming utterly miserable. Also a sun hat, some sun cream and a pair of sun specs. To guarantee comfort, you have to allow for almost anything.

A county cricket match is also a splendid backdrop to do some reading to. Some of the grounds – Fenners in Cambridge, or Canterbury, for example – seem to have been designed for this purpose. It is sometimes worth taking a cushion (although these are often available at the ground) because the seats at cricket matches are not renowned for their comfort.

If you are going to see an international match, you can take a radio with you and listen to the commentary (but make sure that you take headphones: other spectators don't like being disturbed). About half of the spectators these days have a pocket radio to enhance their enjoyment of the day.

What is surprising is that it is much easier to see the players at a cricket match than you would imagine: most new spectators wrongly assume that they will need powerful binoculars. Incidentally, the best seats are usually those that are as near to being behind the bowler as possible – that way it is easier to see the ball, and to see whether it is swinging or spinning – but beware! (see the next section). If you sit side on to the pitch and a fast bowler is bowling, you may find it almost impossible to see the ball from the moment it leaves the bowler's hand to the moment that the batsman hits it.

Why do they shout when I walk past the white screen?

One of the worst crimes of any spectator is to move behind the bowler's arm. Batsmen are very easily distracted, and at the slightest disturbance they will stop play. You can usually tell if

you are in the danger area because you will be in line with the sightscreens – the big white (sometimes movable) things at each end of the ground. It is all right to walk in front of the screen when the bowler is running towards you. In general, though, don't move around until the end of the over, lest you prevent a spectator from seeing what could be a vital incident (like a wicket).

In general, cricket is not a game for screaming and shouting (at least, not outside the boundary). The crowd likes to watch in relative peace and quiet. If watching a game in England, keep your voice down, especially if you aren't talking about cricket, or you will very quickly find that you are attracting glares from all corners. Also, keep quiet as the bowler comes in to bowl – you will hear a hush come over the crowd when this happens, followed by a buzz of conversation as everyone analyses what has just happened.

Approval is usually shown by clapping (see page 103), but cries of 'shot', or 'good throw', or 'well held' are all perfectly acceptable. Chanting, or cries of 'send him off, umpire', are less acceptable, which is not to say that you don't hear them.

Ever since the football World Cup in Mexico in 1986, the Mexican Wave has been a feature of cricket spectating. A Wave usually only starts after half-past three when the spectators have had a chance to down a few cans of beer. It seems to have re-

---

5 FILMS IN WHICH CRICKET FEATURES

- *The Lady Vanishes* (1938) – Hitchcock thriller in which two of the characters are obsessed by wanting to know the Test match score

- *A Yank at Oxford* (1938) – Robert Taylor and Vivien Leigh star in a film in which cricket is one of the eccentricities the American visitor has to come to terms with

- *The Final Test* (1953) – Jack Warner plays a cricketer looking forward to his last match

- *The Go-Between* (1970) – Farmer Ted (played by Alan Bates) is caught by the boy Leo on the boundary

- *Hope and Glory* (1987) – Life in the suburbs during World War II, in which a small boy is taught how to bowl a googly

placed the slow hand clap, which used to be very common. Any part of the ground that refuses to participate in a wave is booed by the instigators. Some people find the Wave a harmless and fun part of watching cricket. <u>Members</u> would disagree. So would the players, since a small movement in front of the sightscreen is nothing compared to the sight of a dirty great wave speeding around you. As a spectator it can be very tempting to follow the crowd and join in a Mexican Wave. My advice would be, if the players are still on the field, don't. It isn't fair.

10

But What Makes Cricket so Special?

So far in this book I have mainly been describing the mechanics of cricket. Now you know what a maiden over and a silly mid off are. So what? Understanding how cricket works does not necessarily explain why anyone should find it interesting, or why it should be different from all the hundreds of other sports and pastimes that exist.

It is true that there are many other interests to which people are addicted, such as stamp collecting, train spotting and dressing up as Elvis Presley. But cricket followers regard themselves as different. They see their interest as being both a recreation and something of a religion; not just something to watch or play, but also to incorporate into the way they behave. (There again, so do people who dress up as Elvis Presley.)

People love cricket for many different reasons. Some like the mental and physical challenge of playing it; others simply enjoy watching it or reading about it, without ever having taken part. Cricket enthusiasts may describe cricket to you as a 'metaphor for life'. They will tell you that they love it for the artistry, or the contests between individuals, or the anecdotes and statistics, or the way that it upholds old-fashioned courtesy, ritual and tradition. Or perhaps what they really love is the commentary on Radio 3.

But perhaps the most important part of cricket is its very English sense of humour, an absolute essential for a game that can so easily be disrupted by rain. The worst mistake that you can make about cricket is to take it too seriously.

For example, perhaps you vaguely remember that in 1991 England beat the West Indies at The Oval. This hadn't happened for many years. The papers were filled with analysis of all the vital statistics, the bold decisions the selectors had taken, the tactics that had been used, the bad shots that were played, the good bowling and the heroic innings.

But did you know that England actually won that match because of a pigeon? It was the Sunday afternoon, the West Indies were fighting back in their second innings, and it looked as if England might be set a big target to win in their second innings. Then a pigeon flew on to the pitch. The batsman (Jeffrey Dujon) stopped the bowler and chased the pigeon away. He settled himself to face again, but the pigeon started strutting back towards him and again he held his hand up. By now, the crowd was in

---

5 ANIMALS THAT HAVE DISRUPTED A CRICKET MATCH

- 1889 Pig stops play, running across the cricket field (Worcestershire v Derbyshire)

- 1936 Sparrow stops play. The ball hit it in midflight and killed it. It is now an exhibit at Lord's (MCC v Cambridge University)

- 1957 Hedgehog stops play, wicket-keeper carefully carries it off the pitch (Gloucestershire v Derbyshire)

- 1957 Mouse stops play, its schoolboy owner runs on to the field to recapture it with his cap (Kent v Hampshire)

- 1962 Bees stop play, players flee to the pavilion to escape (Oxford University v Worcestershire)

hysterics. Again he chased the bird off, and this time he indicated that he was ready for the bowler to bowl. But just as David Lawrence bowled, the pigeon began to strut back towards the pitch, the crowd began to titter, Dujon (almost certainly distracted) edged the ball with his bat and Alec Stewart, the wicket-keeper, jubilantly took the catch. This was a vital wicket and England went on to win the match.

Now I ask you: how can you take a game seriously when a pigeon plays such an important part? When the experts say that cricket is a funny game, they really mean it. *That* is what makes it so special.

Glossary and Index

DON'T PANIC!

You are not supposed to read and learn the contents of this glossary. If you try, you will probably give up cricket for good.

No, this section is here for three reasons:

- AS A GLOSSARY. You will find it essential to carry this book at all times if you are (i) listening to the radio commentary, or (ii) in conversation with a cricketer. A brief description is given for each word. To keep the glossary at a manageable length, I have used cross references (in **bold**). To begin with these will keep you busy flicking from definition to definition (but not, I hope, going in circles).

- AS AN INDEX to the rest of the book. So, for example, if you want to know what a **googly** is, look it up under G, and you will find the page numbers on which reference is made to googlies. If there is no page number and you need to know more, ask a cricket-loving friend.

- AS A THESAURUS. Sometimes there is more than one word to describe something in cricket. For example, the **pitch** can also be known as the **wicket** or as the **batting strip**. I have added the alternative words for each bit of cricket-speak. The most commonly used expression is in most cases the one I have given the full definition for.

There are a staggering 600 cricketing words or expressions in this section (and cricket buffs will delight in telling you the ones that I've left out). I must admit, until I sat down to compile this lot I had no idea just how packed with jargon cricket is. No wonder it seems so incomprehensible to the outsider.

Of the words that I have included, some are common 'official' words (e.g. **third man**); some are common but colloquial (e.g. **tonk**); and many are quite rare (e.g. **chinaman**) – but I put them in just in case.

Colloquial words are marked 'coll'. When it is not clear from context, I have marked nouns as 'n', verbs as 'vb', adjectives as 'adj' and adverbs as 'adv'. Words with more than one meaning are marked [1], [2] etc.

I had to draw the line somewhere, so you will not find in this glossary expressions like 'bowling wicket to wicket', 'beating the batsman with a peach', or 'whipping the ball off his legs'. For the time being, at least, these will have to remain part of the mystery of cricket.

Absent hurt/ill   a member of the batting team does not go out to bat because he has a broken arm, hangover etc. (this effectively counts as a batsman **out** for the team).

Action [1]   The style in which the bowler bowls the ball.

Action [2]   description of which arm the bowler bowls with, and whether he bowls **round the wicket** or **over the wicket**.

Agricultural   a style of batting deemed unorthodox and inelegant – an agricultural shot is usually a **cow shot**, a **tonk** or a **hoick**.

All out   end of a team's **innings** when there is nobody left to bat. 43

All-rounder   player who is a good batsman and a good bowler (usually bats at number six or seven in the **batting order**). 49

All run four   four **runs** scored by running between the wickets four times (usually only managed if there is a very **long boundary** or a slow fielder with a feeble throw).

Allow a single   see **give the batsman a single**.

Anchor   a batsman who plays **defensively** with the intention of batting for as long as possible, so that his partners at the other end can take risks [also **hold one end up**].

Appeal   member of fielding team asks umpire if batsman is **out** ('How is that?, '**Howzat**' etc.) [also **shout**] 38-9, 74

Arm ball   deceptive ball that looks like it will be an **off break** but in fact travels straight on after bouncing. 66

Arrive at the crease   see **come in** [2].

Ashes   a **series** of **Test matches** between England and Australia, named after a very small trophy that contains the ashes of a burnt bail. 92

Asking rate   the average number of runs per over needed by the team batting second in order to win the match (**limited overs** only).

At the wicket/crease   see **in**.

Attack (n)   a description of all the bowlers in a team (e.g. 'they have a very strong attack' – they have a lot of good bowlers).

Attack the batsman   to set an **attacking field**.

Attacking batsman   batsman who is looking to score runs off most of the balls he faces. 51

Attacking bowler   a bowler who is always trying to **take a wicket** (and may not worry about **conceding runs**).

Attacking field   fielders standing close to the batsman looking to pres-

118

surize him and take catches [also **close field**]. 42, 69, 83

Attacking shot   a shot in which the batsman is trying to score runs. 55,56

Average   statistic which indicates how well batsman or bowler has done in the past (batting average is runs per innings, bowling average is runs per wicket). 38

Away swing   see **out swing**.

Back away (vb)   either a batsman's attempt to **make room** to hit the ball, or to avoid being hit by the ball (or both).

Back foot   foot of the **facing batsman** which is nearest to the **wicket-keeper**. 54, 56

Back-lift   the raising of the bat before the batsman attempts to hit the ball.

Back up [1] (vb)   to stop a throw from another fielder (if the **wicket-keeper** or bowler has missed it). Prevents **overthrows**.

Back up [2] (vb)   **non striker** walks forward as bowler bowls, so he will have less distance to run to the other end.

Backward (of square)   any fielding position on the **wicket-keeper**'s side of the stumps [also **behind square**]. 70

Backward defensive   a **defensive** shot. 56

Bad ball   a ball which is unlikely to **take a wicket** and is likely to concede runs, such as a **long hop** [also **loose ball**].

Bad light   light deemed by umpires too dark for cricket to be played safely without endangering the batsmen. 48

Bails   the small pieces of wood which sit on top of the **stumps**. 33

Ball [1]   the round thing they play with, traditionally red: the outer casing is leather and there is a prominent, stitched **seam** around the circumference. 60

Ball [2]   the whole piece of action between the bowler letting go of the ball and the batsman playing it [also **delivery**]. 26

Bat [1] (n)   the wooden thing (always made of willow) the batsman hits the ball with.

Bat [2] (vb)   to be one of the two batsmen you see in the middle of the field. 49

Bat-pad   a shot which hits the pad and the **edge** of the bat.

Batsman   somebody picked for his team because of his skill at batting; also generally anyone who goes in to bat. 26, 49-58, 83

Batting average   see **average**.

Batting crease   the painted white line (or **crease**) on which the **facing** batsman stands. 25, 35

Batting order   the order in which the batsmen in the batting team go in to bat after the **fall** of each **wicket**. 49-50

Batting strip   see **pitch**.

119

Batting wicket   a good quality **pitch** on which batsmen usually score lots of runs.

Beamer   a dangerous ball that passes the batsman above chest height without bouncing; may count as a **no ball** and usually unintentional [see also **full toss**]. 59

Beat (the bat)   description of a ball that makes the batsman **play and miss** e.g. 'that ball beat him outside **off stump**'. 85

Beat the field   batsman hits the ball past a fielder.

Beat in the flight   (of a slow bowler) to deceive a batsman who misjudges speed and trajectory of the ball.

Behind the bowler's arm   any area which is behind the bowler, as viewed by the **facing** batsman. 111

Behind square   see **backward**. 70

Benson & Hedges Cup   a limited overs competition for the county teams. 94

Blinder   an extremely good catch.

Block (n/vb)   **defensive stroke** played with a **dead bat**.

Blockhole   the part of the **crease** where the batsman's bat touches the ground. Where **yorkers** bounce.

Bodyline   description of a bowling tactic used in the 1932/3 **Ashes series** when England's bowlers deliberately bowled **short** and aimed at the batsman's body [see also **leg trap**]. 19, 20

Bosie (coll.)   see **googly**. 67

Bottom hand   batsman's hand which is nearest the main part of the bat (and which puts most of the power into a shot).

Bouncer   ball which bounces half way down the **pitch** and passes the batsman at head height and fearsome speed [also **bumper**]. 58, 61

Boundary [1]   edge of the field of play, marked by a rope, flags, hedge, cliff etc. 29

Boundary [2]   a shot in which the ball crosses the boundary (scoring four or six runs). 29

Bowl (vb)   to hurl the ball with the arm straightened. 17, 58-68

Bowled   one of the ways in which a batsman can be **out** [**played on** is a special case]. 32

Bowler   somebody picked for his team because of his skill at bowling; also generally anyone who bowls. 25, 26, 58-68, 83

Bowler's end   end from which bowler bowls [also **non striker's end**]. 25

Bowling average   see **average**.

Bowling crease   the line on the pitch on which the bowler's **front foot** usually lands. 30

Bowling figures/analysis   the details of what the bowler has done (number of **overs** and **maidens** he has bowled, runs **conceded** and **wickets** taken). 40, 102

Box   protective equipment worn in the jockstrap. 57

Bump ball any shot which looks like a **catch**, but in which the batsman actually hit the ball into the ground before it bounced up.

Bumper (coll.) same as a **bouncer**.

Bye type of **extra**, when ball does not touch anything attached to the batsman and the batsmen run. 31, 76

Call (for a run) the shout of 'Yes', 'No', 'Wait', etc. from the batsman who is in the best position to decide if a run is possible. 36

Carry (vb) a ball which travels within reach of a fielder without bouncing (e.g. 'that **edge** carried to first **slip**').

Carry one's bat an **opening batsman** carries his bat when he remains **not out** while the whole of the rest of his team are **out**.

Catch see **give a catch**.

Caught one of the ways in which a batsman can be **out**. 32, 40

Caught and bowled **caught** by the bowler (usually written 'c & b').

Caught behind **caught** by the **wicket-keeper**.

Century any batsman's score of 100 runs or more. 28, 103

Chance a missed opportunity to take a **wicket** (possibility of **stumping** or a **catch**).

Change bowler bowler who comes on for one or two **overs** to allow another bowler to rest or change **ends**. 83

Channel (coll.)(n) see **corridor**.

Charge (vb) the batsman moves two or three paces along the **pitch** in order to be able to hit the ball hard [more attacking gesture than **use one's feet** or **dance down the pitch**].

Chinaman a special type of bowling by a **left-arm, spin** bowler. 67

Chinese cut a type of **false stroke** where the ball hits the **inside edge** of the bat and just misses the **stumps** [countless other names including **Harrow cut, Surrey drive**].

Chucker a bowler who bowls the ball with a bent arm, or who throws the ball (either of which are officially a **no ball**).

Clean bowled **bowled** without the ball touching any part of the batsman's body or bat first (Most **bowleds** are clean!). 33

Clip (off one's toes) type of shot, usually **half volley** played towards **square leg** [also to **turn the ball off one's legs**].

Close field see **attacking field**.

Close of play end of the day's play (usually six o'clock or six-thirty in a **first class** match) – [also **stumps**]. 89

Collapse (n/vb) a rapid fall of wickets for not many runs. 106

Come in [1] to run up to bowl.

Come in [2] new batsman walking on to the field after the **fall of a wicket** [also **arrive at the crease**].

Come in (off the pitch) [3] what the ball does when it **deviates** towards the batsman [also **move in**]. 64-5

Come in [4]   fielder moves closer to the batsman.

Come in off a short/long run   to have a short/long **run up**. 60

Come off [1]   to leave the field.

Come off [2]   to stop bowling or **finish a spell**. 58

Come on (to bowl)   start a new **spell** of bowling.

Concede runs   to have runs scored off one's bowling (e.g. 'my bowlers conceded a lot of runs today'). 102

Coopers & Lybrand Ratings   computer world ratings of cricketers who play in **Test Matches**, a guide to their more recent Test Match form. (Originally named **Deloittes Ratings**.)

Correct (adj)   describes batsman who plays in an orthodox way [see also **textbook** and **straight bat**].

Corridor (of uncertainty)   anywhere between the batsman's **off stump** and about a foot **outside off stump**. If the ball goes here, the batsman is uncertain whether he should **leave** it or not.

County Championship   the main league played by **first class** counties. 94

County cricket   cricket played by the eighteen **first class** counties. 93-5

Cover   fielding position [also **cover point**]. 69

Cover drive   a type of **drive** shot played towards **cover**. 54, 56

Cover point   fielding position [also **cover**].

Covers   anything used to cover any part of the field to protect it from rain. 47

Cow corner (coll.)   unconventional fielding position between **long on** and **deep mid wicket**. 71

Cow shot   inelegant shot off a **straight ball**, aimed towards **deep mid wicket/cow corner**.

Crease   all painted lines on a cricket pitch are called 'creases' [see **batting crease, popping crease** and **ground**]. 25

Cross (vb)   the batsmen usually cross near the middle of the **pitch** when they take a run. If they cross before a **catch** is taken the **new batsman** starts as **non striker**. 29

Cross bat (shot)   usually an ugly, unsafe shot in which the batsman tries to hit a **straight** ball with his bat horizontal.

Crowd (the batsman) (vb)   to place a lot of fielders in **attacking field** positions.

Cut (n/vb)   type of shot played towards the **off side** with weight on the **back foot**. 56

Dance down the pitch   (of a batsman) to skip elegantly sideways towards the bowler before hitting the ball (risk being **stumped**) [also **use one's feet**]. 35

Danger end   the end of the **pitch** to which the fielder sends his throw and to which one batsman is running.

Dead ball   a moment determined by umpire (usually when ball lands in **wicket-keeper**'s gloves) after which the batsmen aren't allowed to run and cannot be **out** until the next ball is bowled.

Dead bat   very **defensive shot** in which bat is held still, allowing the ball to hit it.

Declare/declaration   formal decision to finish team's **innings** before all the **wickets** have been lost. 43-4, 90

Deep   any fielding position near to the **boundary** (e.g. deep **mid wicket**). 71

Defensive batsman   batsman whose main priority is not to be **out** [extreme cases are known as **stone wallers, blockers**]. 51

Defensive field   fielders not very close to the batsman, who have the main aim of preventing the batsmen from scoring runs. 69, 83

Defensive stroke   an attempt to hit the ball with the intention of not being **out** rather than scoring runs [see also **dead bat**, **forward defensive**].

Delivery   a ball bowled by the bowler [also **ball [2]**].

Delivery stride   the final step of a bowler's run up to bowl.

Deloitte(s) Ratings   original name for the **Coopers & Lybrand Ratings**.

Deviation (n)   Change of direction (after ball hits **pitch** or bat). 64-5

Dig in short   to attempt to bowl a **bouncer**.

Dig out (a yorker)   to hit a **yorker** with the bottom of the bat.

Direct hit   a **throw in** by a fielder which hits the stumps [see also **throw down the stumps**]. 36

Dismiss   see **get out**.

Dismissal   the end of a batsman's innings because he is caught bowled or LBW etc. (see **lose a wicket**, **out**). 32

Dolly (catch)   an extremely easy **catch** to take. Often dropped [also **sitter**].

Dot ball   ball off which no runs of any kind are scored. 101, 102

Double century   a batsman's **innings** of 200 or more runs.

Down the corridor/channel   see **corridor**.

Down the off (leg) side   see **outside off stump**.

Drag on   see **play on**.

Draw (n/vb)   A result of a match in which neither side has won or **tied**. 44, 45-6, 95

Draw stumps   to take the stumps out of the ground, indicating that it is **close of play**.

Drinks (interval)   a formal break, usually half way through a **session**, in which drinks are brought on for the players (only on hot days). 74

Drive   type of shot in which batsman hits ball on the **half volley, forward** of **square**. 56

Drop [1]   fielder moves further away from the batsman [also **move deeper**].

Drop [2]   to miss a **catch** [also **put down**]. 73

Duck (n)   a batsman's score of nought runs (only if he is **out**) [see also **golden duck**, and **pair**]. 28

Economical   said of a bowler who **concedes** relatively few runs.

Economy rate   average number of runs the bowler concedes every **over**.

Edge (n/vb)   type of **false stroke** in which the ball hits the edge of the bat [also **get an edge**, snick, **nick**]. 32

Eleven   alternative name for the cricket team. 97

End   the part of the **boundary** directly behind where the bowlers **run up** (as in 'the Pavilion End'). Also the part of the **pitch** near to the **stumps**. 26

Enforce   see **follow on**.

Expensive   said of a bowler who **concedes** a lot of runs. 67

Extra   any run which is scored when the ball has not hit the bat or glove of the batsman [also **sundry**]. 30-31

Extra cover   fielding position. 69, 70

Extract lift (vb)   to get the ball to bounce high when it hits the **pitch**.

Face [1] (vb)   to be the batsman waiting to have the ball bowled at him [also **receive, take strike**]. 25

Face (of the bat) [2](n)   the flat, front part of the bat with which the batsman tries to hit the ball.

Facing batsman   see **striker**. 25

Fall of wicket   when a batsman is **out** (e.g. the third **wicket** fell at a score of 168).

False stroke   any shot where the ball goes in a different direction from where the batsman intended [also **mishit**]. 86

Farm (the bowling)   to deliberately try to **face** all of the bowling (usually to protect a weak, **tailend** batsman at the other end) [also farm the strike, hog the bowling].

Fast bowler   bowler who projects the ball quickly [also **paceman**, **quickie**]. 58, 60-61, 85

Fast pitch   a **pitch** on which the ball moves quickly after it has bounced [also **lively pitch**].

Field [1] (vb)   to be the team which is doing the bowling and fielding. 67-73, 82

Field [2] (n)   the whole area within the **boundary**.

Field [3] (vb)   to chase, stop, pick-up and/or throw in the ball. 72

Fielder   anyone in the fielding/bowling team except the current bowler and (strictly) the wicket-keeper [also sometimes **fieldsman**]. 67-73

Fifty   batting landmark, any batsman's score between fifty and ninety-nine runs [also **half century**]. 28, 103

Fine (adv/adj)   any fielding position which is close to being directly behind where the **wicket-keeper** stands; any shot which goes in that direction. 71

Fine leg   fielding position. 71

Finish a spell   to complete a **spell** of bowling [also **take one's sweater**].

First class (adj)   an official level of cricket played by certain counties, states etc. (**Limited over** matches are not first class.) 42, 91

First slip   the **slip** fielder who stands nearest to the **wicket-keeper**. 55, 70

Fishing   see **play and miss**.

Five runs   penalty added to batting team's score if ball is stopped or **caught** illegally (e.g. using fielder's cap). 32

Flannels   a cricketer's trousers (no longer made of flannel material). 18

Flash   to attempt to hit the ball very hard (usually only used when batsman **plays and misses** or **edges** the ball).

Flat bat (n/vb)   any unorthodox type of aggressive shot played with the bat horizontal when it hits the ball.

Flight [1](n)   the trajectory of the ball (usually from a **slow bowler**). 86

Flight [2](vb)   see **give the ball air**.

Flipper   trick ball similar to a **top spinner**. 67

Float up (vb)   see **give the ball air**. 65

Floater   same as **arm ball**.

Fly slip   fielding position (a sort of **deep third slip**). 70

Follow on (n/vb)   team is asked to start its second **innings** immediately after finishing its first **innings** because it has not scored enough runs (follow-ons are **enforced**). 45

Follow through [1] (n/vb)   (bowler) where the bowler's feet go for the two or three paces after he has let go of the ball.

Follow through [2] (n/vb)   (batsman) to let the bat continue through its arc after the ball has been hit.

Footmarks   rough patch on the **pitch** where bowler's feet land [also **rough**].

Force (off back foot)   an aggressive shot played with weight on the **back foot**, usually towards the **off side**.

Force (batsman) on the back foot   what a fast bowler does when he bowls **short**.

Forfeit an innings   to **declare** the **innings closed** without going out to bat.

Forward   any fielding position just on the bowler's side of **square**, e.g. forward **short leg**, forward **square (leg)** [also **in front of square**]. 70

Forward defensive   type of **defensive shot** in which batsman puts **front**

foot forward in order to **play** the ball on the **half volley**. 54, 56

Four   a shot counting as four runs in which the ball crosses the boundary, having bounced at least once [also **boundary**]. 29, 76

Front foot   the batsman's foot which is nearest to the bowler; also the bowler's foot which lands nearest to the batsman as the bowler lets go of the ball. 31, 54

Full length   see **pitched up**.

Full toss   a ball which reaches the batsman without bouncing [see also **beamer**]. 59

Gap (in the field)   any space between two fielders.

Gardening   act of the batsman prodding the **pitch** with his bat to flatten a small divot, or to calm his nerves. 88

Gather   (of a fielder) to pick up the ball.

Get an edge   see **edge**.

Get behind the ball   said of a batsman who hits the ball with his bat protecting his body (a sign of a skilled batsman) [opposite of **play away from one's body**].

Get one's eye in   to bat carefully until one is used to the pitch and the bowlers. 26

Get (one's foot) to the pitch of the ball   batsman gets his **front foot** close to where the ball bounces when he plays his shot (hence reducing chance of giving a **catch**).

Get one's head over the ball   a batting technique to avoid giving a **catch**, (see **good technique**).

Get (oneself) out [1]   (of a batsman) to **lose one's wicket**, often by doing something irresponsible. 26

Get out [2]   to finish a batsmans innings by **LBW, caught** etc. [also **dismiss, take (his) wicket**]. 26, 32

Get up   of a ball which bounces higher than normal off the **pitch** [opposite of **keep low**].

Give a catch   to hit the ball in the air towards a fielder.

Give out   umpire raises finger to indicate that the batsman is **out**. 38, 76

Give the ball air   to bowl the ball so that it lobs up quite high and is slightly slower than the normal ball [also **toss up, flight** or **float up the ball**].

Give the batsman a single   place the fielders so that the batsmen can easily take one run if they want to [also **allow a single**].

Give the charge   see **charge**.

Glance   type of shot in which ball is played delicately towards **fine leg** [also **leg glance** and if even finer, **tickle**].

Glide   usually a delicate shot played on the **half volley** towards **third man**.

Glove (vb)   (of a batsman) to inadvertently touch the ball with the glove.

A batsman can be **out caught** off his glove. 32

Go for the runs   (of the team which bats last) to have the intention of winning the match, usually said when team is taking risks [see also **swing the bat**]. 89

Golden duck   an **innings** in which a batsman is **out** for nought on the first ball he **faces**. 28

Good length   ball bounces just short of being a **half volley** (perhaps six feet in front of the batsman), making it difficult to score runs from.

Good line   usually bowling that is aimed at the stumps or just outside off stump, so that the batsman has to play it [also **straight**, see also **corridor** and **make the batsman play**].

Good technique   said of a batsman who bats in a way likely to reduce chance of being **out** to a minimum (usually made up of **straight bat**, **textbook shots**, **get one's head over the ball**, **get behind the ball**).

Googly   a 'trick' ball bowled by a **leg spin bowler** which spins the opposite way to the way the batsman is expecting [also **Bosie**, **wrong'un**]. 19, 67, 68

Grass-cutter   see **grubber**.

Green wicket   a **pitch** with green grass still showing on it, usually making the pitch very **fast**.

Ground (n)   see **batting crease**. 35

Ground one's bat (vb)   place one's bat touching ground within the **crease**, to avoid being **stumped** or **run out**. 35-6

Ground staff   the people who prepare and look after the field; usually several of the ground staff are junior players.

Grubber   ball which does not bounce more than one or two inches off the ground [also **grass-cutter, shooter**].

Guard   the precise position in front of the **stumps** where the batsman holds his bat. 53

Gully   fielding position. 70

Half century   see **fifty**.

Half volley   ball which bounces just before it hits the bat, usually very easy to hit.

Handled the ball   one of the ways in which a batsman can be **out** (very rarely happens). 37

Harrow cut   see **Chinese cut**.

Hat trick   bowler takes three **wickets** in three consecutive balls (which need not be in the same **over**, or indeed match!) [see also **on a hat trick**].

Have a go   see **swing the bat**.

Have time   said of a batsman who appears to have plenty of time to **get into position** before playing a shot [similar to **see the ball early**].

Heavy roller   large (often motorized) **roller**, used to flatten the pitch before the start of a team's **innings**.

Helmet   protective headgear worn by most batsmen, and by fielders at **silly point** or **short leg**. 57

Hit across the line   try to hit ball, which is going **straight** or **down the off side**, towards the **leg side**.

Hit against the spin   risky shot in which batsman attempts to hit a **leg break** towards the **leg side** or an **off break** towards the **off side**.

Hit out   see **swing the bat**. 84

Hit the ball twice   one of the ways in which a batsman can be **out** (extremely rare). 37

Hit through the line   to hit the ball back roughly in the direction it came from (usually a **drive** stroke).

Hit wicket   one of the ways in which a batsman can be **out**. 36, 37

Hoick (coll.)   to play an **agricultural shot**.

Hold its own   of a ball which instead of **deviating** (as might be expected because of a slope on the pitch) keeps going straight.

Hold one's end up   batsman has main aim of not being **out** while his partner at the other end scores runs.

Home (adj).   see **in** [3].

Hook (n/vb)   type of stroke played towards **leg side** when ball bounces above shoulder height. 55, 56

Howzat! (coll.)   see **appeal**. 38

Hundred   see **century**.

Hurried stroke   any shot in which batsman appears to decide to play the stoke at the last second (credit is usually given to bowler) [the batsman does not **have time**].

In [1]   currently batting: 'the batsman is in' [also **at the wicket, at the crease, batting, out in the middle**]. 24, 27

In [2]   has been batting for a long time and is now comfortable (e.g. 'We mustn't give this batsman a chance to get in'.)

In [3]   within the **crease** and safe from the threat of a **run out** (after running) [also **home, safe**]. 36

In front (of the wicket)   see **forward**.

In swing   **swing** that makes the ball drift from **off** to **leg side**. 63

Indoor cricket   a version of cricket played in a gymnasium.

Infield   fielders within, say, 30 yards of the batsman [also men saving the one].

Innings [1]   description of what a batsman has done before he is **out**, e.g. 'he played an exciting innings of 30 runs' [also colloquially a **knock**]. 23, 88

Innings [2]   description of whole team's performance since they started batting (e.g. 'Surrey have so far scored 200 for 3 in their first innings').

22, 40, 42, 44, 91

Innings closed   point at which team finished batting.

Innings victory   see **win by an innings**.

Inside edge   the edge of the bat nearest to the batsman.

Inside the crease   a batsman who has a foot or his bat on the **wicket** side of the **batting crease**.

Interval   a formal break in the play, usually between **sessions** (e.g. **tea**), but also on hot days [see **drinks interval**]. 84, 89

Joke bowler   a bowler who hardly ever bowls.

Keep down   (of a batsman) to hit a ball deliberately downwards so that it bounces well in front of a **close fielder**.

Keep low   opposite of **get up**.

Keep the ball up   to bowl balls which are **pitched up**.

Keep wicket   to be the **wicket-keeper** [also **go behind the stumps** and sometimes **do the timbers**]. 72-3

Keeper   see **wicket-keeper**.

Kill the spin   batting technique to counter-act the potential danger of a spinning ball by playing a **forward defensive**.

King pair   two **golden ducks** for the same batsman in one match.

Knock (coll.)   see **innings** [1].

Last man [1]   the final (usually eleventh) batsman to walk out to bat (so when the next **wicket** falls, the team is **all out**) [see also **rabbit**, **tailender**]. 45

Last man [2]   number of runs scored by player who was **out** at the last **fall of wicket** (usually recorded on the **scoreboard**). 105

Late cut   type of shot played deliberately towards where **first** or second **slip** would be. 55

Late swing   a ball that only begins to **swing** when it gets close to (or sometimes beyond) the batsman.

Laws [of cricket]   cricket doesn't have rules, it has laws. 17

LBW   one of the ways in which a batsman can be **out** [also **leg before wicket**]. 33, 34, 74

Leave (alone)   batsman does not attempt to hit the ball [also **not play it**, **let it go**, **shoulder arms**, sometimes **pad up**]. 26

Leaves the batsman   ball deviates towards the off side in the air or off the pitch, and **beats** the batsman. 65

Left arm (bowler)   bowler who bowls the ball with his left hand. 67

Left hander   batsman whose **bottom hand** on the bat is his left hand. 52

Leg before wicket   see **LBW**.

Leg break   type of **spin** ball which spins from **leg side** to **off**. 65, 67, 68

Leg bye   type of **extra** in which ball hits any part of batsman except his bat or gloves and runs are taken. 31, 76

Leg cutter   type of ball bowled by **medium pace** or **fast bowler** which **deviates** off the **pitch** away from the right-hand batsman. 64

Leg glance   see **glance**.

Leg slip   fielding position. 71

Leg side   half of the **field** (look at the diagram on page 71!) [also **on side**]. 25, 54

Leg spin   the art of bowling **leg breaks, googlies,** and **top spinners** [also **wrist spin**]. 66, 67

Leg spinner   a bowler who bowls **leg breaks** [also **leggie**]. 66, 67

Leg stump   the stump behind the batsman that is nearest to the **leg side**. 34

Leg trap   fielders placed **behind square** on the **leg side** to catch a ball **played off the body** [see also **Bodyline**]. 20

Leggie (coll.)   see **leg spinner**.

Length   see **line and length**.

Let the ball go   see **leave alone**.

Lift   the amount of bounce that a bowler is able to give the ball (e.g. 'he is extracting a lot of lift from the **pitch** today').

Limited overs (match)   type of match in which each side has the same number of **overs** in which to score as many runs as possible [also **one day cricket**]. 20, 43, 91, 95

Line and length   where a bowler makes the ball bounce (line is direction, length is how far in front of the batsman it bounces). 86

Loft (vb)   to hit the ball in the air, usually over the head of **mid** or **mid off** fielders.

Long boundary   any part of the boundary which is a relatively long way from the pitch (similarly **short boundary**).

Long hop   ball which is not very fast and bounces about half way down the **pitch**.

Long leg   fielding position. 71

Long off   fielding position. 70

Long on   fielding position. 71

Loose ball   see **bad ball**.

Loosener   a bowler's first ball (usually inaccurate). 26

Lord's   the main venue for **Test Matches** and cup final matches in England, and the headquarters of the **MCC**, the **TCCB** and indeed cricket itself. 17, 18, 92

Lose a wicket   a batsman is **out**.

Lose by an innings   opposite to **win by an innings**. 45

Lose one's wicket   to be **out** [also **to be dismissed**].

Lower order (batsman) batsman who usually bats at number nine, ten or eleven [also **tailender**]. 52

Lunch interval at the end of the morning **session** of play. The lunch break is usually forty minutes.

Maiden (over) an **over** off which no runs are scored. 26, 40, 102

Make room batsman moves a foot or so in the direction of **square leg** to increase the chance that he can play an attacking shot [also **back away**].

Make the batsman play to bowl accurately so that the batsman has to hit the ball to protect his **wicket**.

Mark the point from which a bowler starts his **run up** (usually he puts a white disc there) [different from **overstep the mark**]. 26

Match abandoned premature finish to a match, usually because of **rain** or riots.

Medium pacer any bowler whose speed is somewhere between slow and fast. 58, 61

MCC Marylebone Cricket Club, exclusive all male club based at Lord's cricket ground, which used to control most aspects of world cricket. 17, 19, 20

Members those who pay an annual subscription to one of the **counties**, entitling them to a seat near the **pavilion**. 113

Mexican Wave popular form of disturbance caused by bored or drunk spectators. 106, 112

Mid off fielding position. 69, 70

Mid on fielding position. 69, 71

Mid Wicket fielding position. 71

Middle, be out in the to be batting [also **to be at the crease, to be in**].

Middle (vb) batsman hits the ball hard, but he hardly feels anything [also **time, hit on the sweet spot**].

Middle and leg a **guard** in which the bat is held at a position in line with his **middle** and **leg stumps** (also **two legs**). 53

Middle order numbers six, seven and eight in the **batting order**.

Middle stump the middle of the three **stumps** behind the batsman.

Minor Counties those English counties which do not play in the county championship. 94

Misfield ball bounces out of, or through, fielder's hands.

Mishit batsman does not hit the ball as hard as, or in the direction that, he intended.

Miss a dropped **catch** or missed **stumping** [also **missed chance**].

Move away of a ball which **leaves the batsman**. 63, 65, 86

Move one's feet batsman's attempt to **get behind the ball** or to **get to the pitch** of the ball.

Movement any **deviation** or swing of the ball after being bowled. 63

Nagging length   description of bowling which consistently pitches on a **good length** [similar to **there or thereabouts**].

NatWest Trophy (National Westminster Bank Trophy)   a sixty-over-a-side knockout tournament for the county teams. 94

Nelson   a score of 111 runs (batsman or team) often deemed to be unlucky. (Also double Nelson etc. Half Nelson is not possible.) 78

Nets   a pitch surrounded by nets where cricketers practise.

New ball   brand new ball taken at the start of each match and each **innings** (which may, if the **fielding** captain wishes, be replaced after a pre-agreed number of **overs** in the innings). 60

New batsman   batsman at the start of his **innings**.

Nick   see **edge**.

Night watchman   usually a **tailender** who comes in to bat in place of one of the better batsman within, say, fifteen minutes of **close of play**. 84

Nip back   what the ball does if it cuts in towards the batsman when it bounces. 65

No ball (n/vb)   illegal ball, usually because bowler's **front foot** lands beyond the **crease**. 30, 31, 71, 76

Non striker   the batsman who stands at the **bowler's end** [see **striker**]. 24, 25

Not out   batsman who is not yet **out** (and might never be). 31-2

Obstructing the field   one of the ways in which a batsman can be **out** (extremely rare). 37, 75

Occasional bowler   bowler who would not expect to bowl in every match (because he isn't particularly good). 89

Off break   type of **spin** ball in which the ball spins from the **off side** towards the **leg side**. 65

Off cutter   opposite of **leg cutter**. 65

Off drive   type of **drive** in direction of **mid off**.

Off (side)   opposite half of the field to the **leg** (or **on**) side (see the diagram on page 70-71). 25, 54

Off spin   the art of bowling **off breaks** (bowled by an **off spin** bowler).

Off stump   the stump behind the batsman and nearest to the **off side**. 34

Off the mark   (of a batsman) to have scored his first run in this **innings**.

Offer the light   ask the batsmen if they want to stop playing because it is getting too dark to see the ball properly (see **bad light**). 48

On a hat trick   the bowler has **taken a wicket** with both of his previous two balls (see also **hat trick**).

On a pair   to have made a **duck** in the first **innings** and not yet scored a run in the second innings.

On drive   type of **drive** in direction of **mid on**.

On (side)   see **leg side**. 54

One day cricket   see **limited overs**.

One day wide   a special **wide** only applicable in **limited overs** matches, where ball goes **down the leg side**.

One short   signal given by umpire to show that one run should be deducted because a batsman failed to run the full length of the **pitch** before running back.

Opening bat(sman)/opener   either of the first two batsmen in any **innings**. 31, 51

Opening bowler   either of the first two bowlers in any **innings**. 60, 102

Orthodox batsman   any batsman whose **stance** and **strokes** would be found in a coaching manual.

Orthodox bowler   usually means the **left arm** equivalent of an **off spinner**.

Out   end of batsman's **innings** because he is bowled, caught etc., at which point he has to leave the field [also **dismissed** and many other colloquialisms]. 23, 26, 32-8, 76

Out swing   **swing** that makes the ball drift towards the **off side**. 63

Outfield [1]   fielders near to the **boundary**.

Outfield [2]   any part of the **field** other than the **square**. 73

Outside edge   type of **false stroke** in which ball hits the edge of bat furthest from the batsman.

Outside off stump   a ball from a bowler which is travelling anywhere on the off side of the batsman's **stumps** (similarly 'outside leg stump') [also **down the off (or leg) side**, see **corridor**]. 34

Oval   any cricket ground in Australia is called an oval; 'The Oval' is a ground in London (now called The Fosters Oval). 92

Over (n)   set of six balls bowled by one bowler. **No balls** and **wides** do not count towards the over. 26, 40

Over (the wicket)   **right arm bowler** runs up past umpire's left hand. 87

Over pitched   ball bounces too close to batsman, making it easy to hit [see also **pitched up, half volley**].

Over rate   the number of overs bowled in an hour (ought to exceed 15).

Overseas player   in England, any foreign player not qualified to play for England.

Overstep (the mark)   (of bowler) to put **front foot** over the **crease** (hence a **no ball**). 31

Overthrows   runs scored because a **throw in** from a fielder is not stopped. 30

Paceman   see **fast bowler**.

Pad   the piece of equipment worn to protect the batsman's legs.

Pad up [1] (vb)   to put on pads before going in to bat.

Pad up [2] (vb)   to deliberately let the ball hit the pads without attempting to hit it (so he cannot be **caught**, although he risks **LBW**) [sometimes same as **leave alone**].

Pair   two **ducks** in one match for the same batsman [see also **king pair**].

Partnership   the length of time spent and number of runs scored by a pair of batsmen before one of them is **out** [also **stand**]. 31-2, 104

Pavilion   building where the players get changed and have tea, and where the **members** can sit.

Penetrate [the field]   see **beat**.

Pick one's spot   (of a batsman) to hit the ball accurately in a particular direction, usually towards a **gap** in the field.

Pick the seam   to use one's fingernails to (illegally) make the ball's **seam** more prominent.

Pick up [1] (n/vb)   the act of a batsman lifting up his bat before hitting the ball.

Pick up [2] (vb)   to deliberately hit the ball in the air (with intention of scoring a boundary) [see also **loft**].

Pick up [3] (vb)   to be able to see the ball against the background (applies both to a batsman and a fielder).

Pick up and throw (n/vb)   usually a tidy, swift piece of fielding all done in one smooth motion.

Pick up runs   see **score**.

Pitch [1] (n)   the twenty-two-yard-long strip of white-looking grass between the two sets of **stumps** [also **wicket**, **[batting] strip**]. 15, 25, 26, 58, 59, 81

Pitch [2] (vb)   to bounce on the **pitch** (e.g. the ball pitches six feet in front of the batsman'). 58, 61, 64

Pitch [3] (n)   where the ball bounces on the pitch (see **get one's foot to the pitch**).

Pitched short   a ball which bounces half way along the **pitch**. 61

Pitched up (adj)   a ball which bounces close to the batsman [also **full length**, may also be a **half volley** and **over-pitched**].

Place (vb)   see **pick one's spot**.

Play (the ball)   to hit the ball with the bat.

Play and miss/play at   attempt to hit the ball with the bat but miss it [also **fish, play down the wrong line**].

Play away from one's body   to **play** the ball without having one's body behind the bat (risky and usually a sign of cowardice).

Play back   batsman moves back towards his **stumps** and plays a defensive shot with bat held vertically. 56

Play for a draw   to bat defensively with no intention of trying to win.

134

Play off one's body   to hit a ball (that would otherwise have hit the torso) **defensively** towards the **leg side** [see also **leg trap**].

Play on   to inadvertently hit the ball on to one's **stumps** [special case of being **bowled**; also **drag on**]. 32

Play oneself in   (of a batsman) to bat carefully until he gets used to the conditions [also **get one's eye in**].

Plug away   to bowl for a long **spell** without much success.

Plumb (adj)   description of an **LBW** that is beyond any doubt.

Point   fielding position. 70

Polish (vb)   see **shine**.

Popping crease   the **batting crease**.

Promote a batsman   to put a batsman higher up the **batting order** than he bats normally (perhaps to make him a **night watchman**). 84

Pudding   see **sticky wicket**.

Pull (n/vb)   type of shot played towards the **leg side** when the ball bounces to about waist height.

Push the ball through   to bowl the ball faster than normal.

Push   type of stroke somewhere between a **forward defensive** and a **drive**.

Put down (a catch)   see **drop**.

Put in (to bat)   after winning the toss, ask opposing team to be the first team to bat. 82

Pyjama cricket   any cricket in which players wear coloured clothing (usually in Australia). 95

Quickie (coll.)   a **fast bowler**.

Quick single, take a   a run taken despite the fact that the ball is hit close to a fielder (risking a **run out**).

Rabbit   player who is absolutely useless at batting (usually batsman number eleven, the **last man** in). 52

Rain (bad light) stopped play   weather interruption of play. 47

Receive   see **face**. 24

Recognized batsman   a player who has a reputation for being competent as a batsman.

Rest day   a break in the middle of the Test match when players go off to rest.

Retired (out)   batsman decides to finish his innings. 37

Retired hurt   temporary end to a batsman's **innings** due to injury etc. 37

Return crease   the lines which are painted on the pitch and are at right angles to the batting or **popping crease**.

Reverse sweep   type of stroke played on bended knee in which batsman

sweeps ball in reverse through the **slip** area (risk of a **top edge**). 55

Right arm (bowler)   bowler who bowls with his right hand.

Right hander   batsman whose **bottom hand** on his bat is his right hand.

Roller   heavy implement used to flatten the **pitch** before each innings.

Rough   a rough patch on the **pitch** caused by **running on the pitch**, which helps the ball to spin [see also **footmarks**].

Round arm   bowling with the arm horizontal rather than vertical, these days only adopted by bowlers who can't get their arms as high as they used to. 17

Round the wicket   **right arm bowler** runs in past umpire's right hand. 87

Rubber   see **series**.

Run   means by which the batting team increases its total **score** (usually achieved by hitting ball with the bat and running to other end of the **pitch**). 23, 29

Run on the pitch   when batsman or bowler run on the **pitch** where the ball is likely to bounce: an offence for which they can be warned because it can be used to deliberately create **rough**.

Run out   one of the ways in which a batsman can be **out**. 22, 36

Run rate   the average number of runs being scored each **over**.

Run up   the route taken by the bowler as he runs up to bowl. 26, 60

Run up!   cry from batting team or spectator to tell batsmen to run more quickly.

Runner   if a batsman is unable to run because of injury, he may ask a member of his team to be a runner, i.e. to do the running for him.

Safe   see **home**.

Safe shot   any stroke which carries little risk of the batsman being **out**.

Saving the single   any fielding position which makes it hard for a batsman to score a run if it goes towards that fielder.

Sawdust   sawdust put on the **pitch** or the **run ups** if they are wet (following rain).

Score [1](n)   the number of runs made and **wickets** lost by the team so far during current **innings**. 31, 104, 105

Score [2](vb)   to make runs. 29-32

Score [3](vb)   to keep a record in a book of what happens on every ball of the match. 101

Scoreboard   the board on which the **total** and other details are displayed for all to see [also **telegraph**]. 104, 105

Scorebook   the book in which someone keeps details of the **score**. 101, 102

Scorecard   card on which to keep details of who scored what, and which **wickets** were taken. 40, 80

Scorer   the person who keeps all the details of the match in the **scorebook**. 31, 101

Scoring rate   same as **run rate**.

Seam (n/vb)   stitching around the circumference of the ball which sometimes makes the ball bounce awkwardly. 60, 64

Seam bowler   bowler who often makes the ball land on the **seam** when it hits the **pitch**. 58, 64

Seamer   same as **seam bowler**; also the type of delivery that a seam bowler bowls. 58, 64

See the ball (early)   said of a batsman when he appears to be playing with great ease.

Selectors   the group of men who pick the country's team.

Series   two or more **Test matches** played between two countries over a period of two or three months (usually three or five matches) [also sometimes called **rubber**, see **Ashes**]. 92

Session   period of play between start of play and lunch, lunch and **tea**, or tea and **close of play**.

Set the field   (usually the captain) tell fielders where to stand. 67, 83

Shine   to make one half of the ball shiny so that it will **swing** in the air [also **polish**]. 61-3

Shooter   see **grubber**.

Short [1](adj)   a ball which bounces at least ten feet in front of the batsman who is **facing** (shorter than **short of a length**). 61

Short [2](adj)   any fielding position closer to the batsman than is the convention (e.g. 'short **third man**').

Short arm (jab/pull)   description of a type of aggressive shot played with little **back lift** or **follow through** and the elbows kept close to the body.

Short boundary   see **long boundary**.

Short leg   fielding position [can also be '**forward** short leg' or '**backward** short leg']. 69, 71

Short of a length   a ball which bounces about ten feet in front of the batsman (who plays it off the **back foot**).

Short run [1]   a run which is disallowed because batsman runs back without touching his bat inside the **crease** at the other end [see also **one short**].

Short run [2]   a bowler's shortened **run up**, especially a tactical ploy of a fast bowler who usually has (or **comes in off**) a long run up. 60

Shot   see **stroke**.

Shoulder arms (vb)   to deliberately avoid hitting the ball by lifting the arms and bat above one's head.

Shout (coll.)   see **appeal**. 38-9

Sightscreen   light coloured screen placed on the boundary behind bowler's arm so that the batsman can see the ball (usually white with slats in it so it isn't blown over). 87, 111

Signal   sign made by the umpire to the **scorer** to show what has happened. 31, 76

Silly   fielding position within three or four yards of the batsman (silly **point**, silly **mid on** and silly **mid off**). Silly because it is so dangerous. 69, 70, 72

Single   see **take a single**.

Sitter   an easy catch, similar to a **dolly**.

Six   shot counting as six runs because the ball crossed the **boundary** without bouncing. 29, 76

Sledging   a mean tactic (adopted by **close fielders**) of whispering taunting or racist remarks at the batsman.

Slip(s)   fielding position(s) (can be **first**, second, third, fourth, **fly**, **leg**, and, very rarely, fifth). 32, 70

Slog (n/vb)   an inelegant shot played with feet nowhere near the ball, attempting to hit a six; also **swing the bat**.

Slow bowlers   usually bowlers with a **run up** of only three or four paces. 65-8, 89

Slow pitch   opposite of **fast pitch**.

Slower ball   a sneaky **delivery** in which a fast bowler bowls with his usual **action** but deliberately makes the ball go slower to deceive the batsman. 87

Snick (n/vb)   see **edge**.

Solid batsman   a batsman who gives few **chances** and who generally **gets behind the ball**. 51

Sound (adj)   said of a batsman who has **good technique**.

Specialist (batsman/bowler)   a player picked for the team because he is a good batsman/bowler.

Spell   the **overs** bowled by a bowler from one **end** until he is replaced by another bowler. 58

Spinner   type of slow bowler who makes the ball **deviate** when it bounces [also **spin bowler**]. 58, 66-8

Splice (n)   the part of the bat where the handle joins the wide bit.

Square [1] (adv/adj)   any fielding position which is side on to the batsman so that the fielder can only see one **stump** from where he stands. 71

Square [2] (n)   the rectangular, well kept area of grass in the middle of the **field** (one strip of which is the **pitch**).

Square cut   type of **cut** stroke played **square** on **off-side**. 54, 56

Square leg   fielding position. 69, 71, 74

Stance   the body position of the **facing** batsman. 53

Stand   see **partnership**.

Stand back   what the **wicket-keeper** is doing if he stands more than two or three feet behind the **stumps** when the bowler bowls. 70

Stand up   what the **wicket-keeper** is doing if he stands just behind the **stumps** when the bowler bowls.

Sticky wicket   a very wet **pitch** which is difficult to bat on [also sticky dog, **pudding**].

Stock bowler   a bowler relied on to bowl a lot of **overs** in one day. 61

Stone waller   see **defensive batsman**.

Stop   of a ball which appears to slow down and bounce higher when it hits the pitch.

Straight [1]   to bowl straight is to bowl the ball straight at the stumps. 26, 87

Straight (bat) [2]   an orthodox or classical way of playing one's **strokes**, with the bat vertical and the bat face towards the bowler when playing a **defensive shot**.

Straight [3] (adv/adj)   any fielding position close to being **behind the bowler's arm** (or shot which goes in that direction).

Streaky runs   runs scored in a lucky fashion (usually off the **edge** of the bat).

Strike bowler   a bowler who has a good **strike rate**; any fast or threatening bowler renowned for **taking wickets** regularly.

Strike rate   the average number of balls a bowler bowls between taking **wickets**.

Striker   the batsman at whom the bowler is bowling [also **facing batsman**]. 24, 25

Stroke   the method and direction in which the ball is hit [also **shot**, sometimes **hit**]. 56

Strokeplayer   a batsman who usually plays attacking, elegant shots. 51

Stump [1] (n)   one of the three sticks at both ends of the pitch (three stumps plus bails make up the 'wicket', sometimes 'timbers'). 15, 32, 34

Stump [2] (vb)   (of a **wicket-keeper**) to **get** a batsman **out, stumped**. 35

Stumped   one of the ways in which a batsman can be **out**. 35, 40

Stumps (n)   see **close of play**.

Sub(stitute)   any player who comes on to replace one of the eleven players in the team (see **twelfth man**). 74

Sunday League   limited overs competition for counties. 94, 109

Sundries   the Australian term for **extras**. 30

Sweep (n/vb)   type of shot played towards the leg side on bended knee [also sometimes 'paddle']. 56

Sweeper   fielding position (usually adopted in **limited overs** cricket). 70

Swing [1] (n/vb)   (of a bowler) to make the ball swerve in the air. 58, 62, 63

Swing [2] (vb)   (of a batsman) to attempt to hit the ball hard, usually aiming towards **deep mid wicket**.

Swing the bat   to attempt to score as many runs as possible as quickly as possible with little regard for the risk of **losing one's wicket** [also **have a go, hit out, slog** and sometimes **go for the runs**].

Tailender   batsman who bats late in the innings and is not very good [also **lower order batsman** and, if he's very bad, **rabbit**]. 52

Take a single   score one run by running to the other end of the pitch.

Take a wicket   **get out** a batsman. 26, 28, 40

Take guard   see **guard**.

Take off (a bowler)   (of the captain) to **finish** a bowler's **spell**.

Take one's sweater   see **finish a spell**.

Take spin   said of a pitch if a spin bowler is able to make the ball **deviate** when it bounces. 66

Take strike   see **face**.

Take the stumps   (of anyone in fielding team) to stand next to the **stumps** ready to catch a throw in.

TCCB   Test and County Cricket Board, governing body of cricket which deals with sponsorship, playing regulations etc. in the UK.

Tea   interval between playing sessions in late afternoon. 98

Technical chance   a missed catch or stumping which only Superman could have taken.

Telegraph (coll.)   see **scoreboard**.

Test (match)   international match between two countries of **Test status**, which lasts up to five days. 19, 91-3

Test status   countries which are deemed good enough to be allowed to play official **Test matches** (there are now eight of them). 92

Textbook shot   a shot which anyone who teaches cricket would be proud of. 55

There or thereabouts (coll.)   said of a bowler who bowls **line and length**.

Thick edge   type of **false stroke**, usually safe (i.e. the ball goes along the ground), in which ball goes off part of the bat near to its edge.

Thigh pad   protection worn on the thigh. 57

Thin edge   an **edge** that is very faint causing tiny deflection of the ball.

Third man   fielding position. 70, 72

Throat ball (coll.)   dangerous form of **bouncer** which rears up towards batsman's throat. 20

Throw (vb)   to bowl with a throwing action (i.e. with a bent arm), a **no ball**.

Throw down the stumps   (of a fielder) to throw the ball and hit the stumps (usually while the batsmen are taking a run) [also **direct hit**]. 36

Throw in (n/vb)   a throw from a fielder towards the **stumps**.

Tickle (n/vb)   a **glance** that is hit very **fine**.

Tie   the result of a match in which the teams score the same number of runs and the last team to bat are **all out**. 44

Tight bowling   accurate bowling which it is hard to score runs off [similar to bowling **line and length** and likely to be **economical**].

Timbers   see **stump**.

Time (vb)   see **middle**.

Timed out   very rare type of **dismissal**, intended to prevent time wasting by the batting team. 37

Tonk (coll.)   to hit the ball hard.

Top edge   a type of **false stroke** when the batsman fails to play a **square cut** or **hook** off the middle of the bat.

Top hand   batsman's hand which is furthest from the main part of the bat.

Top spinner   a ball that looks like it will be a **leg break** but instead goes straight and bounces higher. A close relative of the **googly**. 67

Toss (n/vb)   Toss of coin to decide which team bats first. 24, 64, 81

Toss up (vb)   see **give the ball air**.

Total   Number of runs scored so far by the team in the current **innings**; also the final number of runs scored by the team at the end of the innings. 28, 31, 40, 106

Tread on one's wicket   usually of a batsman who inadvertently falls back and kicks his stumps (and is thus **out**, **hit wicket**).

Trundler (coll.)   an unthreatening, slow to **medium pace** bowler.

Turn   the amount by which the ball **deviates** from a straight line when it bounces. 68

Turn the ball off one's legs   any shot played upright in which the batsman hits a ball that was going to hit his legs in a direction which is towards or **behind** the position of **square leg**.

Twelfth man   the main substitute fielder. 74

Two (legs) (coll.)   same as **middle and leg**.

Umpires   the two men in white coats who control the play on the cricket **field**. 24, 25, 48, 74-8

Underarm   type of bowling style now almost extinct. 17-18

Unorthodox   any **stroke**, fielding position or other aspect of play which would not be found in the coaching manuals. 55

Upper cut   unorthodox type of **cut** stroke in which batsman deliberately hits the ball over the heads of the **slips**.

Use one's feet   see **dance down the pitch**.

Vacant (area)   part of **field** where no fielder is standing [also **gap**].

Victim   a batsman whom a bowler has got out, e.g. 'he claimed five victims' [also **wicket**].

Walk (vb)   batsman decides he is out before waiting for umpire's decision (very honourable thing to do). 39

Walk in   (of fielders) to walk towards the batsmen as the bowler runs up to bowl. 97

Wicket [1] the **dismissal** of a batsman. 15, 28, 32-8, 40

Wicket [2] the set of three **stumps** at either end of the **pitch**. 15

Wicket [3] another word for **pitch**. 15

Wicket maiden an **over** in which no runs are scored and the bowler **takes a wicket**. 102, 103

Wicket-keeper the fielder with gloves who stands behind the **stumps** [also **keeper**, sometimes 'wickie']. 25, 49, 70

Wickets left number of **wickets** that have to fall before the team is **all out**. 43

Wide type of **extra** in which ball cannot be hit by the batsman because it is out of his reach [see also **one day wide**]. 30, 76

Wide mid off fielding position less **straight** than **mid off** (similarly 'wide **mid on**', 'wide first **slip**' etc.).

Win what happens to a team if it doesn't lose, draw or tie the match. 41-5

Win by an innings a win in which the winning team only has to bat once, while the losers bat twice [also **innings victory**]. 44

Win by x wickets to win by overtaking the score of the opponents with *x* **wickets remaining**. 43

Wisden Cricketers' Almanack a fat, annual reference book which contains details of all the **first class** cricket played in the world. 107

World Cup a four-yearly competition played by the major cricketing countries. The matches are all limited overs. 95, 97

World Rating computer rating of **Test** cricketers [see **Coopers & Lybrand Ratings**]. 51

Wrist spinner see **leg spinner**

Wristy description of a batsman who twists and turns his wrists when he hits the ball.

Wrong 'un see **googly**.

Yahoo (coll.) a batsman's wild swing at the ball (usually he misses it).

York (vb) to bowl a **yorker**.

Yorker a ball which bounces on or very near to the batsman's toes, and is very difficult to hit. 86, 88

Some Selected Further Reading

This is a small handful of the thousands of cricket books that have been written. Several of them have been valuable references in writing this book.

For a pleasant, historical account of cricket:

> *Double Century, The Story of MCC and Cricket*, Tony Lewis, Hodder & Stoughton, 1987

For a deeper, more philosophical analysis of cricket:

> *Beyond a Boundary*, C L R James, Stanley Paul, 1963 (many reprints)
>
> *The Art of Captaincy*, Mike Brearley, Hodder & Stoughton, 1985

For easy-to-read and amusing cricket anecdotes:

> *Test Match Special*, edited by Peter Baxter, Unwin, 1981
>
> *This Curious Game of Cricket*, George Mell, Unwin, 1983
>
> *Fine Glances – A Connoisseur's Cricket Anthology*, edited by Tom Graveney and Mike Seabrook, Simon & Schuster, 1990

For all sorts of records, rules, facts and figures:

> *Wisden* (any year from 1864 onwards)
>
> *Who's Who of Cricketers*, Bailey, Thorn & Wynne-Thomas, Newnes, 1984

Cricket's Strangest Matches, Andrew Ward, Robson Books, 1990

Next Man In, Gerald Brodribb, Pelham Books, 1985

For those condemned to cricket widowhood:

Cricket Widows (mainly cartoons), Noel Ford, Angus & Robertson, 1989

Bluff Your Way in Cricket, Nick Yapp, Ravette Books, 1986

Another Bloody Tour, Frances Edmonds, Kingswood Press, 1986